MW00480091

Man of Fire

William Tecumseh Sherman in the Civil War

by Derek D. Maxfield

EMERGING CIVIL WAR SERIES

Chris Mackowski, series editor
Cecily Nelson Zander, chief historian

The Emerging Civil War Series

offers compelling, easy-to-read overviews of some of the Civil War's most important battles and stories.

Recipient of the Army Historical Foundation's Lieutenant General Richard G. Trefry Award for contributions to the literature on the history of the U.S. Army

Also part of the Emerging Civil War Series:

For a complete list of titles, visit
https://www.savasbeatie.com/civil-war/emerging-civil-war-series/

Man of Fire

William Tecumseh Sherman in the Civil War

by Derek D. Maxfield

EMERGING CIVIL WAR SERIES

Savas Beatie
California

© 2023 by Derek D. Maxfield

All rights reserved. No part of this publication may be reproduced, stored in
a retrieval system, or transmitted, in any form or by any means, electronic,
mechanical, photocopying, recording, or otherwise, without the prior written
permission of the publisher. Printed in the United States of America.

First edition, first printing

ISBN-13: 978-1-61121-599-1 (paperback)
ISBN-13: 978-1-61121-600-4 (ebook)

Library of Congress Cataloging-in-Publication Data

Names: Maxfield, Derek D., author.
Title: Man of fire : William Tecumseh Sherman in the Civil War / by Derek D.
    Maxfield.
Other titles: William Tecumseh Sherman in the Civil War
Description: El Dorado Hills, CA : Savas Beatie, [2023] | Series: Emerging Civil
    War series | Includes bibliographical references and index. | Summary: "By turns
    he has been called a savior and a barbarian, a hero and a villain, a genius and a
    madman-but whatever you call William Tecumseh Sherman, you must admit he
    is utterly fascinating. Forging an identity in the fire of war, the unconventional
    general proved to everyone at Shiloh, Vicksburg, Chattanooga, Georgia, and in
    the Carolinas that, while he was unorthodox, he was also brilliant and creative.
    More than that, he was eminently successful and played an important role in
    Union victory"-- Provided by publisher.
Identifiers: LCCN 2021055997 | ISBN 9781611215991 (paperback)|
    ISBN 9781611216004 (ebook)
Subjects: LCSH: Sherman, William T. (William Tecumseh), 1820-1891.| United
    States--History--Civil War, 1861-1865--Biography. | Generals--United States--
    Biography. | United States. Army--Biography.
Classification: LCC E467.1.S55 M347 2022 | DDC 355.0092--dc23/
    eng/20211116
LC record available at https://lccn.loc.gov/2021055997

SB

Published by
Savas Beatie LLC
989 Governor Drive, Suite 102
El Dorado Hills, California 95762
Phone: 916-941-6896
sales@savasbeatie.com
www.savasbeatie.com

Savas Beatie titles are available at special discounts for bulk purchases in the United
States by corporations, institutions, and other organizations. For more details,
e-mail us at sales@savasbeatie.com, or visit our website at www.savasbeatie.com for
additional information.

For Jess

Table of Contents

Table of Contents

(continued)

List of Maps

Maps by Edward Alexander

$\mathscr{A}$cknowledgments

I suppose it is only appropriate, when acknowledging those that aided or influenced the present work, to begin with General William Tecumseh Sherman. I have spent so much time with him that I feel like we are friends. By leaving behind such an extensive written legacy, the historian enjoys an embarrassment of riches. As I have wrestled with the darker, less admirable aspects of the general's life, I have also learned much about myself. Sherman has guided and challenged me; for this, I am grateful.

This is my second book published by Savas Beatie. Of course, I owe much to Ted Savas, my publisher, for supporting my work. But, I also owe a debt of gratitude to the magnificent team at Savas Beatie—and an apology. In the acknowledgments of my first book, *Hellmira: The Union's Most Infamous Civil War Prison Camp—Elmira, NY*, I failed to thank "the

William T. Sherman founded the Command and General Staff College at Fort Leavenworth, Kansas, but Sherman Army Air Field, located there, is actually named after a different William Sherman, Major William Carrington Sherman, who wrote the army's first airplane tactics manual. (ar)

SB Ladies." In particular, I have been aided most generously by Sarah Closson, Sarah Keeney, Lois Olechny, and Veronica Kane.

I continue to owe an incalculable debt to my friend and editor, Chris Mackowski, at Emerging Civil War. That he continues to work with me on my writing projects is a wonder, despite my pestering. I am also grateful for the help of Sarah Bierle, also at ECW, for supporting my blog posts and reading an early draft of this work. Another ECW alum, Dave Powell, generously wrote the forward for the book, despite heavy commitments. I sincerely appreciate Dave lending me his name—and with it considerable dignity.

One of the joys of this particular project is its collaborative nature. All the appendices were written by Genesee Community College partners—Jess Maxfield, Tracy Ford, and Michael Gosselin. Each make unique and invaluable contributions with their essays and are excellent added value for the reader. I deeply appreciate their contributions.

Finally, this modest volume is, in part, possible because of the success and interest in *Hellmira*. I wish to thank all those who bought copies of that work, corresponded with me about it, hosted book talks and signings, and generally made me feel like my time mattered. I will always be grateful.

PHOTO CREDITS: Angela Riotto (ar); Chris Kolakowski (ck); Chris Mackowski (cm); Genesee Community College (gcc); George Hettenhouse (gh); *Harper's Weekly* (hw); Library of Congress (loc); Kristen Trout (kt); Public domain (pd); Derek D. Maxfield (ddm); Missouri Historical Society (mhs); National Archives (na); New York Public Library (nypl); Terry Rensel (tr); Wikipedia Commons (wc); Wikipedia Commons/King of Hearts (wc/kh)

For the Emerging Civil War Series

Theodore P. Savas, *publisher*
Chris Mackowski, *series editor and co-founder*
Cecily Nelson Zander, *chief historian*
Sarah Keeney, *editorial consultant*

Maps by Edward Alexander
Design and layout by Veronica Kane

Foreword

By David Powell

Excepting Abraham Lincoln, William Tecumseh Sherman might be the most recognizable Civil War figure of them all, even including Robert E. Lee and Thomas J. "Stonewall" Jackson. Everyone knows, after all, that Sherman "burned Atlanta," and "made Georgia howl!" They may not know how or when, but very often, they know who. Certainly, he garners far more name recognition than his friend and superior, Ulysses S. Grant.

He is also a favorite subject for authors. My shelves boast no less than eight different biographies of the man, not including his memoirs and a volume of his collected correspondence. Other titles focus on specific campaigns or aspects of his career—and I by no means have all the titles written about him. One reason for this enduring popularity among historians is his prolific and unfiltered correspondence, filled with hasty, often blunt sentiments: all fertile territory for an author. Sherman tended to write before he thought, wearing his opinions on his sleeve. It is the literary equivalent of catnip to a writer. Contrast Sherman with his own friend and close subordinate, George H. Thomas, who was so closemouthed that he instructed his wife to burn his private correspondence upon his death. Thomas's wife obeyed his wishes, much to the chagrin of an entire historical community.

Not so Sherman. His personal and professional correspondence is a treasure trove of opinion and insight. Take, for example, the death of his favorite son in the fall of 1863, just before he traveled to Chattanooga. Willie had taken ill while the family was

In Sherman's hometown of Lancaster, Ohio, a small park at the corner of Main and Front streets features as its centerpiece a bronze statue of Sherman sculpted by Michael Major and unveiled on July 2, 2000. (gh)

visiting Sherman at Vicksburg, dying of fever in the Gayoso Hotel in Memphis. Sherman blamed himself for exposing Willie to the dangers of a deep South climate during the sickly season. In the days following his young son's demise, he recounted how he felt haunted at every turn in the hotel and how Willie, his favorite (he made no bones about that), would now never fulfill the dreams and hopes Sherman had invested in him. Grief is, of course, always deeply personal, but no reader can fail to be struck by the openness of Sherman's feelings.

Moreover, Sherman is central to the story of the war. He commanded a brigade at First Bull Run and finished the war second only to Ulysses S. Grant, commander of the entire Federal Army. Few would have predicted that Sherman would be there at the end, let alone ranked above all save Grant. Rarely an optimist, Sherman predicted a long and bitter struggle, so much so that he was relieved of command at Louisville, Kentucky, after having a bit of a nervous breakdown in the fall of 1861. Yet he found his place under Grant, cementing a reputation for courage under fire at the battle of Shiloh the next April.

He would go on to serve as Grant's right arm during the subsequent siege of Vicksburg, launching some of the earliest assaults against that fortress on May 19 and 22, 1863; and later was assigned the crucial role of keeping the Rebel Army of Relief off his boss's back while Grant went about the bloody business of reducing the stronghold. When Grant arrived in Chattanooga that October, to find that this time a Federal army was nearly besieged and in peril, Grant summoned his fellow Ohioan Sherman to come help. When he arrived, Grant placed all his trust in Sherman's attack against the Confederate positions atop the north end of Missionary Ridge; when Sherman stumbled, Grant re-wrote the narrative to spare Sherman embarrassment. Nor would Grant hesitate to place Sherman in command of the entire Military Division of the Mississippi (embracing the Departments of the Cumberland, Tennessee, and Ohio) in 1864 to lead the great western offensive while Grant himself traveled east to face Robert E. Lee in Virginia.

This brings up another fascinating aspect of Sherman's military career: his dislike of battles and his relative lack of tactical skills. Sherman's forte was logistics and operational maneuver, not tactical

The Sherman House Museum in Lancaster, Ohio, is the birthplace of the general and his younger brother, John, who went on to become a United States senator. The house is listed on the National Register of Historical Places. (gh)

expertise. As a result, Sherman conducted the Atlanta Campaign much differently than Grant conducted the Overland Campaign. Sherman's Georgia campaign was marked by maneuver and skirmishing, rather than slugfests, made all the more so because his opponent for the first half of that campaign was the careful and cautious Confederate General Joseph E. Johnston; by contrast, Grant, in Virginia, went toe-to-toe with perhaps the most aggressive general of the war. Grant and Lee painted a bloody swath from the Rappahannock to Richmond, piling up nearly 120,000 casualties (78,273 Union, 41,138 Confederate) in the space of two months, May through June of 1864. By contrast, over a slightly longer period (May to 17 July), Sherman suffered 21,925 losses, while his opponent Johnston lost 14,213: a total of about 36,000, less than a third of the toll in Virginia. Even the combined Federal and Confederate losses for the full campaign to the fall of Atlanta on September 2nd amount to just under 70,000 killed, wounded, and missing. Lee stopped Grant, but at a horrendous cost. Johnston failed to stop Sherman, and was replaced by Gen. John Bell Hood, who also failed to keep the Federals at bay. Sherman marched into Atlanta and nearly gutted the Army of Tennessee. These were remarkable feats for a general not noted as a tactician. While there were missteps along the way—Kennesaw Mountain, for one—Sherman achieved his objectives.

Of course, Sherman's chief claim to infamy is in what happened after Atlanta: the March to the Sea and into the Carolinas. Memory and the acolytes of the Lost Cause turned Sherman's movement through Georgia from Atlanta to Savannah into a parade of plunder and destruction, akin to "Total War;" the reality was much less dramatic. Sherman's men did live off the land, but as much destruction was caused by Confederate cavalry under Maj. Gen. Joseph Wheeler, practicing a scorched earth policy ahead of Sherman, as was inflicted by Sherman's dreaded Bummers. The March to the Sea is another of those contradictions that comprise the man's character. Even though he is portrayed as the unflinching destroyer, Sherman also granted amazingly generous surrender terms to Johnston in April 1865, so generous that they were repudiated by the Federal government and had to be renegotiated.

Nor do the contradictions cease there. Sherman famously hated politicians and newspapermen. And yet, he was brother to a U.S. Senator (John Sherman), stepson to the politically powerful Ewing clan of Ohio, and law partner to a member of the McCook family, another highly influential Ohio family. And despite his avowed dislike of politics, Sherman was not above pulling those political strings when needed.

His rabid hatred of the press is famous. He was once quoted as saying, "I would kill every reporter in the world, but I am sure we would be getting reports from hell before breakfast." However, he was not above talking to reporters; Sherman didn't hate the press. What he hated was bad press. Given how he was ridiculed early in the war and how some reporters howled for his head after the battle of Shiloh, this should come as no surprise.

This then is Sherman. A mediocre tactician with an operational flair; a merciless opponent in war; and a man of liberal terms in peace. He despised politics but had some of the strongest political connections in the Army—far stronger than Grant's own not inconsiderable support. Sherman was a man who never seemed to think before he spoke or wrote, but worked hard to polish his own reputation in his postwar memoirs—even at the expense, at times, of both his fellow officers and of the truth.

Derek Maxfield's biography of this fascinating man is a welcome addition to the literature, providing us an accessible overview of Sherman's nature.

Sherman Hall at the Command and General Staff College at Fort Leavenworth memorializes the former General in Chief of the Army.
(ar)

Given the format of this series, tackling a subject as complex and contradictory as William T. Sherman is no easy task, and Professor Maxfield's work cannot be described as definitive—but can any work dealing with such a complex figure be considered definitive? I think not, as the draft of previous works clearly demonstrates.

In his conclusion, Professor Maxfield argues that those complexities are what make Sherman both "compelling and fascinating." I agree, and further argue that this volume succeeds in presenting Sherman's complexities in an understandable fashion, furthering our ongoing fascination with him. I am sure readers will agree, whetting appetites for more of "Uncle Billy" Sherman.

DAVID POWELL is the award-winning author of the acclaimed Chickamauga trilogy, *The Chickamauga Campaign* (Savas Beatie) and two books in the Emerging Civil War Series on the Chattanooga campaign, *Battle Above the Clouds* and *All Help Can't Stop Them*.

SHERMAN
A SOLDIER'S PASSION FOR ORDER
John F. Marszalek

Introduction

My association with General Sherman dates back about 25 years to when, as an undergraduate at SUNY Cortland, my mentor Dr. Ellis Johnson fired my imagination with his compelling stories of the Civil War. I will never forget his lectures which featured a double slide projector, music—some of which he played on guitar or banjo, and books—so many books.

At Doc's suggestion, I slogged through Shelby Foote's *The Civil War: A Narrative*, Lloyd Lewis's *Sherman: Fighting Prophet*, and Sherman's own *Memoirs*. I was hooked. And even while my career as a historian seemed to drift in other directions, every time a Sherman book came to hand, all other reading paused.

The book that made me want to become a Sherman scholar was *Sherman: A Soldier's Passion for Order* by John F. Marszalek. This scholarly treatment introduced to me the subtleties of the complex man. His argument that the redhead's life was defined by a need for order intrigued me. Marszalek's brilliant biography has become a pillar in the edifice of my obsession.

To my mind, Sherman's depth and continual search for identity is compelling. Losing his father at a young age began his quest to discover who he was. Taken in by Thomas Ewing, his father's best friend, he lived very near his mother. Whose son was he? The relationship with Ewing would be another source of tension. He loved him and craved Ewing's approval but came to resent him for interference in his own family life. Later, Sherman married Ewing's daughter Ellen—who was both quasi-sister and wife. This in

Historian John Marszalek's *Sherman: A Soldier's Passion for Order* set the standard for Sherman biographies and made a huge impact on author Derek Maxfield. (cm)

Dr. Ellis "Doc" Johnson and the author working on the former's Civil War collection at SUNY Cortland. (ddm)

turn introduced religious tension and Ellen's lifelong attempt to bring Sherman fully into the Catholic fold.

Professionally, the eccentric young man entered West Point at the behest of Thomas Ewing and found he liked soldiering. It suited him. But once he acquired the taste for it, Sherman battled to stay in the service and find his place. When the Mexican War commenced, the redhead desperately wanted to get into combat and earn glory but was denied and ended up in California on administrative duty. His friends, like Ulysses S. Grant, were becoming heroes, and he wasted away, far from the action.

At the bidding of the Ewings, Sherman reluctantly left soldiering behind to try his hand at civilian employment. He worked as a banker, a lawyer, an administrator, a military academy superintendent, and a streetcar operator. A mixture of bad luck and bad timing kept the ambitious young man on the move and trying desperately to find himself.

The Civil War changed everything, though not at first. It did, eventually, give him the opportunity to rejoin the military. He needed to be his own man and prove himself. Soldering was something he knew and a way to fight to preserve the Union—which he loved. But finding his place and his identity within the war took time.

Pablo Picasso famously said, "Every act of creation is first an act of destruction." This seems well suited to understanding Sherman's Kentucky crisis. There, newspapers and some of his colleagues branded him "insane." He was nearly destroyed. Phoenix-like, though, he rose from the ashes and created a new military life and reputation. The battle of Shiloh made Sherman a hero and forced people to reassess their perceptions of the general. From there, the Ohioan took flight.

Second only to Ulysses S. Grant, Sherman became the preeminent hero of the Union war effort. Through determination and perseverance, the voluble commander demonstrated that there was a thin line between insanity and genius. His innovations— best exemplified by his famous March to the Sea—

suggested that the conqueror of Atlanta was no ordinary man. Moreover, it suggested to Sherman that he had made a place; he had forged an identity in the flames of war.

Sherman was truly a "Man of Fire." But not for his famous reputation among partisans as a torch-wielding arsonist—which is overblown—but because the fiery redhead had fire-in-the-belly courage, scorching intellect, smoldering passion, and blazing convictions. His restless energy and intensity literally exhausted, even burned out, those who encountered him. He was a force of nature.

There is much in Sherman's search that I can identify with. A restless spirit, impelled by a need to prove himself, is captivating. That he overcame near annihilation, and utter humiliation, to become a powerful, confident, and lauded hero of the republic is more—it is inspiring.

I hope you enjoy his story.

Fought near Pittsburg Landing on the Tennessee River, the battle of Shiloh takes its name from a little log church a few miles from the landing. (loc)

"You might as well appeal against a thunderstorm as against these terrible hardships of war. War is cruelty, there is no use trying to reform it; the crueler it is, the sooner it will be over."

— William Tecumseh Sherman

Prologue

As he stepped onto the wharf at City Point, Virginia, Maj. Gen. William Tecumseh Sherman could see that the whole area buzzed like a beehive. It was late March 1865, and he had arrived at what had become the Union army's nerve center to see his chief, Lt. Gen. Ulysses S. Grant, whose headquarters was just up the hill in a small cabin on the grounds of the Eppes Mansion.

After a grueling campaign through the Carolinas, a trek of more than four hundred miles, Sherman's army had reached Goldsboro, North Carolina, where it had been strongly reinforced and started the process of refitting and resupplying. Now, the fidgety redhead decided to confer with Grant in person about the coming spring campaign.

The last time the generals had met was about a year earlier, just after Grant had been promoted to Lieutenant General and General-in-Chief. Conferring in Cincinnati, they had discussed Army operations for 1864. The result of that conversation had laid the strategy for the previous year. Sherman and his three field armies went after Confederate General Joseph E. Johnston and his army, then at Dalton, Georgia. Grant travelled with the Army of the Potomac as it pursued General Robert E. Lee's Army of Northern Virginia. Their campaigns had been successful, and the end of the war loomed close.

As the generals met on the wharf at City Point that spring day in 1865, it was a warm reunion. "Their encounter was more like that of two school-boys coming together after a vacation than the meeting

Grant's headquarters at City Point became the focal point of the Union war effort in the final weeks of March 1865. Sherman, Porter, Meade, and others converged to meet with Grant and Lincoln. (tr)

Home of Dr. Richard Eppes, Appomattox Manor became the nerve center of the Union army near Petersburg and the headquarters of Lt. Gen. Ulysses S. Grant. (tr)

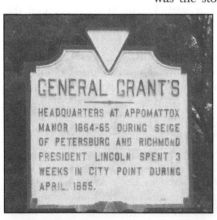

Historical marker remarking on the significance of the Grant headquarters site at City Point. (ddm)

of the chief actors in a great war tragedy," Lt. Col. Horace Porter recalled. An unusual friendship, forged in war, had grown between the two Ohio men. They had met first at West Point, but their contact there was limited. The serious trials of war in the West kindled the friendship under the most trying conditions.

The two men could not be more different in personality and demeanor. Standing about 5'7", Grant was the stoic one. Reticent, reserved—almost shy—the General-in-Chief was nonetheless a keen observer, decisive, exceedingly brave, and cool under fire. One observer described the general as an "ordinary, scrubby-looking man, with a slightly seedy look, as if he was out of office on half-pay." Far from the intellectual that Sherman was, Grant's character reflected a simple, solid man that had unwavering confidence in success.

Sherman stood 5'11" with a straight posture. Well-read, the redhead had a fondness for Shakespeare and was something of a philosopher. He was "Sandy haired and gaunt, with a grizzled, short-cropped beard" and had a nervous manner that some found disquieting. His dark, direct gaze could be intimidating, combined with a "veritable volcano

Grant's headquarters cabin on the grounds of Appomattox Manor at City Point, Virginia, can be visited today. Managed by the National Park Service, the beautiful site sits at the confluence of the James and Appomattox Rivers. (ddm)

of verbiage" that could tax the patience of those he engaged with. Still, the general was gregarious and had a "shoot-from-the-hip sincerity." In short, "Uncle Billy"—as his soldiers dubbed him—was a complex man.

Greeted by Mrs. Grant at headquarters, Sherman settled in with Grant and his staff around a campfire to discuss the plans for 1865. At the front of the cottage, the confluence of the Appomattox and James Rivers made a magnificent scene. Soon, the loquacious general regaled the assembled group with the exploits of his armies. "The story, told as he alone could tell it, was a grand epic related with Homeric power," Porter remembered. "Never were listeners more enthusiastic; never was a speaker more eloquent."

The ebullient storyteller talked about the burning of Atlanta, incidents during the March to the Sea, Christmas in Savannah, the watery slog through South Carolina and the fiery visit to Columbia. The "bummers" had caught the attention of the newspapers and the imaginations of the Northern people, and Sherman wanted to make it clear that "they were not stragglers or mere self-constituted foragers," the general argued, "but there are organized for a very useful purpose from the adventurous spirits who are always found in the ranks. They served as 'feelers' who keep in advance and on the flanks of the main columns, spy out the land, and discover where the best supplies are to be found."

Grant had invited a few high-ranking officers, including Maj. Gen. George Meade, who commanded the Army of the Potomac, to visit with Sherman while he was there. But no one ranked higher and more a

Lt. Col. Horace Porter was an aide on the staffs of both Maj. Gen. William Tecumseh Sherman and later Lt. Gen. Ulysses S. Grant. Porter would also serve as Grant's private secretary when he became president and, in 1897, would be appointed the U.S. Ambassador to France. (loc)

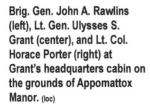

Brig. Gen. John A. Rawlins (left), Lt. Gen. Ulysses S. Grant (center), and Lt. Col. Horace Porter (right) at Grant's headquarters cabin on the grounds of Appomattox Manor. (loc)

VIP than the president himself. "I'm sorry to break up this entertaining conversation," Grant broke in when Sherman finally took a breather, "but the President is aboard the *River Queen*, and I know he will be anxious to see you. Suppose we go and pay him a visit before dinner." Soon, the group broke up, and the pair of generals headed down to the wharf.

Sherman recounted the visit with the president in his memoirs. He said they

found Mr. Lincoln alone, in the after-cabin. He remembered me perfectly, and at once engaged in a most interesting conversation. He was full of curiosity about the many incidents of our great march, which had reached him officially and through the newspapers, and seemed to enjoy very much the more ludicrous parts—about the "bummers," and their devices to collect food and forage when the outside world supposed us to be starving; but at the same time he expressed a good deal of anxiety lest some accident might happen to the army in North Carolina during my absence.

Maj. Gen. William T. Sherman had developed such a strong partnership with Grant over the war that historian Charles Bracelen Flood called it "The friendship that won the Civil War." (loc)

Mrs. Grant had tea ready when Sherman and Grant returned to headquarters. The former wished immediately to talk about the coming campaign. "Perhaps you don't want me here listening to all your secrets," Julia said wryly. "Do you think we can trust her, Grant?" Sherman said, amused. "I'm not so sure about that, Sherman," Grant answered. The trio continued to banter playfully for some time before dinner was announced.

The celebrated *River Queen* conference continued the next day when Rear Admiral David Dixon Porter joined the generals and Lincoln. The tone of this gathering was more serious and business-like than the previous day. Grant informed the group that Maj. Gen. Phil Sheridan would arrive soon, and strike against Lee's only remaining supply line, the Southside and Danville Railroad. "Matters were drawing to a crisis," he observed. There was some concern that Lee might try to escape before Sheridan launched the attack, and the Army of Northern Virginia might try to join with Johnston's army in North Carolina. Sherman assured the group he could hold the combined force if Grant came along in short order.

Julia Dent Grant was the wife of Ulysses S. Grant. She was also a cousin of Confederate General James Longstreet. (loc)

Grant and Sherman agreed that "one or the other of us would have to fight one more bloody battle, and that it would be the *last*." At this, Lincoln stirred and wondered if it was really necessary. "There had been blood enough shed." That would not be up to them, Sherman observed. The president's manner touched the redhead, who remembered later: "I was more than ever impressed by his kindly nature, his deep and earnest sympathy with the afflictions of the whole people, resulting from the war."

At this juncture, apart from the military strategy and tactics necessary to force the surrender of Lee and Johnston, Sherman wanted to know "if [Lincoln] was ready for the end of the war? What was to be done with the rebel armies when defeated? And what should be done with the political leaders, such as Jeff. Davis, etc.? Should we allow them to escape, etc.?"

LEFT: Maj. Gen. George G. Meade was the longest-serving commander of the Union Army of the Potomac. Born in Cádiz, Spain, in 1815, he was raised in Pennsylvania. (loc)

RIGHT: Abraham Lincoln was the 16th President of the United States. As a young man back in Illinois, Lincoln was also a champion wrestler. (loc)

The Peacemakers, a famous painting by George P. A. Healy, was produced in 1868 and depicts a famous wartime meeting aboard the U.S. Navy steamer *River Queen* at City Point, Virginia, in March 1865. From left are Maj. Gen. William Tecumseh Sherman, Lt. Gen. Ulysses S. Grant, President Abraham Lincoln, and Rear Admiral David Dixon Porter. (loc)

Lincoln said he was ready and had just been waiting for the surrenders. He anxiously desired to get the rebels to lay down their arms and go home. As for the political leaders, the president answered with an anecdote, which Sherman "inferred that Mr. Lincoln wanted Davis to escape, 'unbeknown' to him."

One thing that Lincoln communicated very clearly, as observed by both Sherman and Porter, was that he "was willing that the enemy should capitulate on the most favorable terms" (interestingly, in Grant's memoirs, Grant does not write about the *River Queen* conference at all). "Sherman was finding that the President saw eye to eye with him in his desire to give prompt mercy and generosity to the enemy as soon as they laid down their arms." The general and admiral alike recalled that the president "authorize[d] [Sherman] to deal with civil authorities in North Carolina." In fact, in the fall of 1864 Lincoln had then wired Sherman and encouraged him to hold "peace parlays" with the governor of Georgia and even Confederate Vice President Alexander Stephens.

It is significant that Lincoln specified authorization for Sherman and Grant to entertain peace terms for both civic and military affairs at the *River Queen* conference because later, Secretary of War Edwin

LEFT: **Maj. Gen. Philip Henry Sheridan served as both an infantry and cavalry commander during the war. Short of stature, standing only 5'5", Sheridan was impulsive and had a fiery temper.** (loc)

RIGHT: **Confederate General Robert E. Lee was the son of Revolutionary War Maj. Gen. Henry "Light Horse Harry" Lee III. In 1831, Robert married Mary Custis, who was the great-granddaughter of Martha Washington.** (loc)

Stanton would castigate Sherman—even brand him a traitor—for offering Johnston lenient terms and dealing with civic affairs. But, of course, by then Lincoln was dead.

"To Sherman President Lincoln came as a revelation," Lloyd Lewis observed. "He seemed to have "charity for all, malice towards none," Sherman recalled, "and, above all, an absolute faith in the courage, manliness, and integrity of the armies in the field." He was also intrigued by the president's body language. "When at rest or listening, his legs and arms seemed to hang almost lifeless, and his face was care-worn and haggard; but the moment he began to talk, his face lightened up, his tall form, as it were, unfolded, and he was the very impersonation of good humor and fellowship."

Sherman departed for North Carolina at about noon on March 28. The president, concerned that Johnston might do something unexpected, urged his subordinate to get back to his army as soon as possible. To alleviate these fears somewhat, Porter sent the general home in the steamer *Bat*—a faster boat. "We parted at the gangway of the River Queen," Sherman remembered of Lincoln, "and I never saw him again."

Rear Admiral David Dixon Porter was the adoptive brother of David G. Farragut and, after the Civil War, would become only the second full admiral in the U.S. Navy. (loc)

The Ewings's Sherman

CHAPTER ONE
1820–1840

Cadet Sherman, a mischievous young soldier, held the reputation as "the best hash maker at West Point." Although it was strictly prohibited, the redhead regularly smuggled food from the mess hall or other venues to host after-hours banquets in his dorm room. Partly a means to enjoy the company of his fellows, these informal hash dinners also helped to compensate for the terrible meals furnished by the academy—which were mainly boiled and bland.

In June 1836, the wide-eyed Ohioan arrived at West Point to begin his military education. A long way from his home in Lancaster, he was something of "an untamed animal just caught in the far West." His adopted father, Thomas Ewing, had arranged for Sherman's appointment to the academy, and the new plebe wanted to make Ewing proud.

The Ewing family had informally adopted William Tecumseh Sherman when he was just nine. The sixth child of Charles R. Sherman and his wife Mary (nee Hoyt), Sherman was born on February 8, 1820. Charles, who seemed "to have caught a fancy for the great chief of the Shawnees," chose the unique middle name for his third son.

A distinguished attorney, Charles was elevated to the Ohio Supreme Court in 1821. While riding circuit in 1829, the senior Sherman took ill at Lebanon "with a severe chill." He lingered with a fever for several days. Meanwhile, when things appeared critical, Mary received the news and started the trek of more

West Point Military Academy with a view of the equestrian statue of George Washington.
(loc)

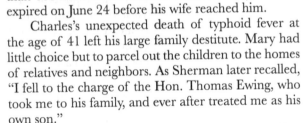

This painting by Andrew Melrose depicts the Hudson River with West Point in the distance. (loc)

than 100 miles to his bedside. Unfortunately, Charles expired on June 24 before his wife reached him.

Charles's unexpected death of typhoid fever at the age of 41 left his large family destitute. Mary had little choice but to parcel out the children to the homes of relatives and neighbors. As Sherman later recalled, "I fell to the charge of the Hon. Thomas Ewing, who took me to his family, and ever after treated me as his own son."

"A lawyer by profession," historian James Lee McDonough wrote, "Ewing was a formidable character, both physically and intellectually." He and his wife Maria (nee Boyle) built a house just a few doors away from the Sherman abode atop a fine hill. Ewing had been close friends with Judge Sherman and often traveled with Charles on the judicial circuit. It is not surprising then that Ewing quickly stepped forward to help when his friend suddenly died.

Already familiar with the Ewing children who had been his playmates for years, young Sherman fit seamlessly into the big house on the hill. Among the seven children were Philemon, who remained a good friend of the energetic newcomer, and Ellen—then only five years old—who would someday become Sherman's wife.

While Sherman had all the Ewings's love and support, there was one troublesome wrinkle—religion. Raised Protestant, William Tecumseh—often called "Cump" for short—found that Maria Ewing had one

Charles Robert Sherman was William Tecumseh Sherman's father. During the War of 1812, the elder Sherman served as a major in the Ohio militia. (wc)

stipulation regarding his entrance to her household: he must be baptized Roman Catholic. Mary Sherman agreed to this, and the deed was done, thereby beginning a contentious thread that ran through the rest of his life and profoundly shaped his marriage to Ellen.

Thomas Ewing's ever-expanding reach and position was another significant influence on Sherman's life. Appointed by the Ohio state legislature to the U.S. Senate in 1830, Ewing became a player in national affairs. Of Whig sensibilities, which rubbed off on his teenage ward, Ewing now hosted political giants who strode through Lancaster, making quite the impression on Cump. Henry Clay, Daniel Webster, William Henry Harrison, and other prominent citizens visited the Ewing parlor.

The Ewing clan always valued education and paid tuition at private schools to ensure their children had quality instruction. Sherman benefited from this vision. In fact, Thomas Ewing seemed to have particularly high aspirations for his charge. From his perch in the Senate, Ewing sent letters instructing his wife to see to the intellectual life of his brood. "He instructed Maria to gather the children around the table at home," Marszalek wrote, "and have Cump and Phil take turns reading from the nine volumes of S. G. Goodrich's Peter Parley books he sent them—volumes that emphasized geography, history, morality, order and American superiority, teaching lessons while they entertained."

Later in life, reflecting on his education, Sherman boasted that the Lancaster Academy "was the best in the place; indeed, as good a school as any in Ohio." The curriculum in those days focused heavily on languages, including Latin, Greek, and French. History and mathematics filled out the program of study, first under the charge of "Mr. Parsons; he was succeeded by Mr. Brown, and he by two brothers, Samuel and Mark How."

As a teenager, Sherman discovered he was destined for West Point. Of course, since Thomas Ewing now sat in the Senate, he had appointments at his disposal. It may be that Philemon had also been slated for a spot at the academy, but he declined. Hugh Ewing suggested that his brother "had aspirations to the priesthood, a more honorable profession than that of a soldier." However, Philemon later told his children that he declined the appointment because he

Henry Clay of Kentucky was a respected American statesman who served as speaker of the House, U.S. Senator, and candidate for president on several occasions. He served as secretary of state to President John Quincy Adams. (loc)

Called the "God-like" Daniel for his powerful oratorical skills, Daniel Webster was a Massachusetts senator with sketchy ethical standards. (loc)

President William Henry Harrison has the distinction of being the chief executive with the shortest tenure of office: just 31 days. Medical historians now believe he died from typhoid fever. (loc)

wanted to study law. In any case, this opened the way for Sherman, who was told to prepare. "Tell Cumpy that I want him to learn fast," Ewing told his wife in a letter home, "that he may be ready to go to West Point or to college soon."

Although Sherman had shown no particular interest in military service, he accepted Ewing's vision as his own and began earnest preparations. "During the autumn of 1835 and spring of 1836," the aspiring cadet wrote, "I devoted myself chiefly to mathematics and French, which were known to be the chief requisites for admission to West Point." Nothing would be more humiliating for Cump and his sponsor than to get an appointment and then be found wanting academically and declined admission.

Spring brought with it the expected appointment. In May, Sherman set out for Washington, D.C., his first stop on his way to the Point. There, the young Ohioan spent a week with Senator Ewing and sightseeing in the Capital. "I think I saw more of the place in that time than I ever have since," Sherman recalled in his memoirs. "General Jackson was President and was at the zenith of his fame. I recall looking at him a full hour, one morning . . . as his paced up and down the gravel walk on the north front of the White House," the future general wrote. "He wore a cap and an overcoat so full that his form seemed smaller than I had expected." Despite his Whig predilections, the sight of Old Hickory, the hero of New Orleans, transfixed Sherman, who silently gazed on the old warrior.

After stops in Philadelphia and New York to see family and friends, Sherman proceeded via steamboat up the Hudson River. Anxiety and a bit of trepidation must have mingled in the wiry redhead when he reached the wharf below the Point. Told to proceed up to the plain, Sherman and the other plebes climbed the hill to find a grand panorama as they caught their breath. High on a bluff overlooking the Hudson River, West Point sits on a grand plain. The old stone buildings— then as now—lend a dignity to the institution. The beauty and majesty of his new surroundings probably inspired awe in the new cadet and his fellows. Writing to Ellen Ewing, Sherman wrote, "Is not West Point worth visiting? Is not the scenery of the finest order in the world? Are there not incidents in its history that render it dear to us all?" Clearly, the child of the West was inspired as he opened a new chapter in his life.

While Sherman learned to love the military life, it posed problems, too, as the independent-minded young cadet adjusted to new expectations and requirements. The rigid dress code, for instance, was burdensome and a bit archaic. In fact, during his tenure at the Point, this kept the Ohioan from attaining an officer's rank. "Neatness in dress and form, with a strict conformity to the rules, were the qualifications for office," Sherman lamented, "and I suppose I was found not to excel in any of these."

One of the earliest educational institutions in Ohio, the Lancaster Academy was also known as Greenfield Academy. The building here existed for just over a decade. (loc)

Discipline at West Point was strict. A system of demerits, in part, determined a cadet's fate. The accumulation of too many could lead to expulsion. One could get demerits from slovenly dress, out-of-bounds drinking, talking after hours, and for many other reasons. According to Marszalek, "Cump averaged more than ninety demerits per year." He "was hardly a model soldier, but he never tried to be. Minor misconduct that earned demerits was unimportant to him."

The program of study at West Point leaned heavily on language and science. Cadets studied math, French, drawing, chemistry, rhetoric, and more. It was expected that this curriculum would fit the men to be fine Army officers. But "when he graduated, Cump was better prepared to be a civil engineer than he was to be a soldier." Pondering his standing in a letter to his brother John, Sherman wrote, "I think I will have about the same standing as I have now in Mathematics and French, but in drawing I think I will be among the first five."

Perhaps the friendships with his comrades were the greatest result of Sherman's tenure at the Point. A social animal, the young man was generally liked and respected—though "many recall him as extremely outspoken and opinionated, sometimes to the point of being offensive." His energy and intensity were manifest, and his nervous manner put off some. William Irwin, a fellow Ohioan, was probably the eccentric redhead's best friend at the academy. Other associates included such Civil War luminaries as Braxton Bragg, George Thomas, P. G. T. Beauregard, James Longstreet, and—when Cump was in his senior year—Ulysses S. Grant, who was called Sam. However, since Sherman was a senior and Grant just a plebe, they interacted very little. In time, a fantastic friendship between the two would shape the very course of the Union's destiny.

President Andrew Jackson was a duelist of note. He killed one man in a duel and carried a bullet in his body for many years as the result of the deadly practice. (loc)

LEFT: The younger brother of William T. Sherman, John Sherman became a member of Congress and was appointed U.S. Senator from Ohio at the start of the Civil War. (loc)

RIGHT: Maj. Gen. George Thomas was a native of Virginia who decided to remain loyal to the Union when his home state seceded. Most of his family never forgave him. (loc)

Known for his mischievous nature, Sherman loved a prank. William Rosecrans recalled with pleasure Cump's antics at the Point:

> *He was always ready for a lark and usually he had a grease spot on his pants from clandestine night feasts. He was the best hash-maker at West Point. Food at the table was cheap and poor and we stole boiled potatoes in handkerchiefs and thrust them under our vests; we poked butter into our gloves and fastened them with forks to the under side of the table until we could smuggle them out of the dining room as we departed. We stole bread and when we got together at night "Old Cump" would mix everything into hash and cook it on a stew pan over the fire. We ate it hot on toasted bread. We told stories and at this, too Sherman was the best.*

After four years of study, Sherman graduated West Point, sixth in a class of forty-three. He would have finished fourth but for his demerits. This did not trouble him, and he took pride in his accomplishments. "In studies I always held a respectable reputation with the professors," Sherman recorded in his memoirs, "and generally ranked among the best, especially in drawing, chemistry, mathematics, and natural philosophy." He would always be proud of being a West Pointer and later, when the Civil War placed him in a position to choose officers, he invariably looked to fellow graduates of the Point.

Graduation meant more than advancement; it meant a furlough, and Sherman eagerly scampered home to relax—and to reconnect with Ellen Ewing, who by now was more than an adopted sister. He began to see her as a love interest. New horizons

Pierre Gustave Toutant-Beauregard was a Confederate general who commanded the Charleston, South Carolina, forces that fired on Fort Sumter in 1861. He was a good friend of Sherman's. (loc)

beckoned, and the newly minted Second Lieutenant readied for the challenges ahead.

One of the more formal pictures of Ulysses S. Grant, this photo is thought to be from 1844 when he was assigned to the 4th U.S. Infantry at Jefferson Barracks in St. Louis, Missouri. (pd)

A Soldier's Way

CHAPTER TWO
1840–1852

Now a West Point graduate, Sherman enjoyed an Ohio respite before reporting for duty in his new station. Because of his class standing, the newly minted officer did not qualify for the Corps of Engineers—the elite class of the Army. Instead, he commissioned as a second lieutenant in the U.S. Artillery, Company A. Once he reached his destination, Florida, he would serve in the closing chapter of the Second Seminole War.

After a whirlwind summer, the eager young artilleryman reported for duty in September 1840. From New York Harbor, he set out for Florida, mostly a tropical wilderness at the time, and Fort Pierce. Sherman found the weather pleasant in his new home and enjoyed much time fishing and swimming. His duties centered around the post with occasional forays against the Seminoles.

Sherman saw little action himself. His one notable escapade involved the capture of Coacoochee, a Seminole chief. In a tense showdown, "Sherman rode directly up to the chieftain and his twelve warriors in their tropical village, and bluntly bade them surrender." During the confrontation, which fixed the attention of the natives, Cump's men quietly gathered all the weapons lying about. After that, there was little difficulty taking them into custody.

A promotion to first lieutenant helped to somewhat compensate for the boredom of his duty at Fort Pierce. An unusual phenomenon to be

Fort Moultrie, located on Sullivan's Island in South Carolina, was decommissioned after World War II and is now operated by the National Parks Service.
(ddm)

Photo of William Tecumseh Sherman as a U.S. Army lieutenant. Sherman sported a ginger red chin beard, but shortly after grew a mustache. (loc)

Coacoochee was a Seminole Chief, better known as Wild Cat. During the Second Seminole War, he was an emissary for Chief Osceola carrying a message to the U.S. Army. (pd)

promoted so quickly—a wait of five years or more was typical—Sherman probably benefited from friends in high places. After all, Thomas Ewing had been a prominent senator and then Secretary of the Treasury under Presidents Harrison and Tyler. At any rate, the promotion meant a new post near St. Augustine, where he found a vibrant social scene.

Sherman's new responsibilities included commanding a company of guards. In a letter to his brother John from his post in Picolatto, he wrote, "I was of course rejoiced at being promoted to this company, which guards the road between St. Augustine and this place,—the road upon which so very many murders have been committed during the war." He felt pleased with his new quarters and the ability to communicate readily with the outside world, but especially the prospect of visiting the old Spanish city. "St. Augustine, you know, is the oldest town in the United States," the young lieutenant wrote, "nor does it's [sic] appearance belie its age—narrow, winding streets, close-built houses with the balconies meeting overhead, denoting its Spanish population." Clearly, Cump enjoyed the old-world charms where there was "dancing, dancing, and nothing but dancing, but not such as you see in the north. Such ease and grace I never before beheld."

In the years immediately prior to the Mexican War, Sherman was stationed near Charleston, South Carolina, on Sullivan's Island. Service at Fort Moultrie was regular and a bit tiresome, but social life offered exciting and lively diversion. A social animal at heart, Lt. Sherman comfortably mingled with the social elite, though now he leaned about the eccentricities of the southern version. The first families of Charleston were an aristocratic set much impressed with their own importance and style. While pretense was never something Sherman admired, he also needed the entertainment and diversion from garrison life.

One of Cump's pleasures at Fort Moultrie was his friendship cultivated with Capt. Robert Anderson, commander of Company G, Third U.S. Artillery. Son of a Revolutionary War veteran, Anderson was a Kentucky-born regular married to a Georgia girl. An artillery specialist, the West Point grad whiled away hours translating French artillery texts. He also avidly collected art, which endeared him to his red-haired subordinate. Sherman became a regular guest in Anderson's home. This bond forged in South

Built in 1838 and abandoned a short time after the end of the Second Seminole War, Fort Pierce was designed as a supply depot for the army. The site of the fort is now a park near the Indian River. (wc)

Carolina would later lead to Anderson choosing his friend as his second-in-command in Kentucky during the Civil War.

Another experience that would pay dividends during the War of the Rebellion arrived at the behest of Col. Sylvester Churchill, the Army's inspector general. Tasked with investigating old Seminole War legal claims, Sherman's new duty took him to Marietta, Georgia, and later to Bellefonte, Alabama. Restless as always, the new inquisitor spent much time in the saddle exploring the Atlanta area, Kennesaw Mountain, and northwest Georgia. Though he did not know it then, his sightseeing turned out to be leisurely reconnaissance. Because Sherman had a remarkable memory and a critical eye for topography, this time mucking about in the red clay would someday prove valuable. "Thus by a mere accident," Sherman recalled in his memoir, "I was enabled to traverse on

Fort Marion, also known as Castillo de San Marcos, is the oldest masonry fort in the continental United States. Built by the Spanish in Saint Augustine in 1676, it was designed to protect the settlement and Spanish claim to Florida. (loc)

The first Fort Moultrie was constructed of palmetto logs and sand, but by 1809 the fort was made with bricks. (loc)

horseback the very ground where in after-years I had to conduct vast armies and fight great battles."

In 1843, Sherman enjoyed a five-month furlough. Of course, he visited Ohio, where family and friends warmly welcomed him. But it was the extended trip back to duty in Charleston at the end of his break that really affected Cump's outlook. He wanted to see the Mississippi River in all its glory. So instead of heading east, Sherman found his way to St. Louis before descending the Father of Waters.

Although Sherman would always remember Ohio fondly, increasingly he would be drawn to the Gateway City. In fact, Marszalek asserts, "His lifelong love affair with St. Louis developed when he first saw the city on this trip." St. Louis fascinated him, and throughout his life, he returned again and again. It became the place he turned to in times of trouble and when he needed a respite from the world. In a real sense, though he was always a wanderer, it became home. And later, it would be where his bones would be laid.

Much like his study of Georgia, which was a matter of simple interest at the time but would have incredible import later, Sherman's sightseeing on the Mississippi also foreshadowed the days when he would command legions of men in this region. He visited Memphis, Vicksburg, and New Orleans and took detailed notes of all he saw. When he finally returned to duty in December, Cump had much to think about, including his vow, "I will never marry."

Apparently, the wiry ginger-haired soldier decided the time had come to propose marriage to Ellen. It is hard to say what exactly led Sherman to this conclusion—though it may have been hormones. "The first thing I will expect of you will be to mount the wildest horse and charge over the hills and plain," Cump wrote his foster sister just prior to his furlough. More than a recreational suggestion, the language of the letter could be read figuratively with sexual connotations.

Victorian custom dictated that the hot-blooded lieutenant first ask Ellen's father, Thomas Ewing, for his daughter's hand in marriage. This delicate proposition had to be handled carefully since there was a degree of almost incestuous feeling about the relationship. While true that Sherman and Ellen were not biologically related, their upbringing under the same roof made them virtually brother and sister. It is quite likely that Ewing and his wife Maria anticipated Cump's proposal and gave it serious thought. It must have been clear to everyone in that household that the pair were in love.

Likely during his furlough, Sherman and Ellen came to an understanding about their relationship and eventual marriage. His application to her father went better than feared—he gave his blessing without condition. However, later when Cump received a letter from Ellen formally accepting his proposal, that did seem to come with provisos. She expected him to leave the military behind and find suitable civilian employment, that they would make their home in Ohio close to her family, and most importantly that he would embrace Catholicism. While these conditions

In the early 20th century, the Cherokee people inhabited the land around Kennesaw Mountain. A gold rush in Georgia paved the way for Cherokee removal under President Andrew Jackson. (wc)

LEFT: Eleanor "Ellen" Ewing Sherman in a portrait by G.P.A. Healy, 1868. (loc)

RIGHT: Maria Wills Boyle married Thomas Ewing in 1819. After the death of her mother when she was only four years old, Maria was raised by her Aunt Susan and Uncle Philemon Beecher. (loc)

should have sent up red flags by the dozen, Sherman promised to "examine with an honest heart" the question of faith. As for giving up the Army and living in Ohio, those were out of the question.

The relationship between these two strong and willful individuals has long intrigued historians. Apart from the obvious affection the two had for each other, their marriage was always a struggle. Sherman wanted to forge his path without the help of the Ewings; he would not be dependent. Something of a gypsy, he never could stay in one place for long. He had to be on the move and loved to travel. He found Ohio boring. As for religion, no greater irritant existed in Cump and Ellen's relationship. She was devout, and he was ambivalent. For the entirety of their marriage, Ellen never gave up her effort to fully bring him into the faith. He fought every step of the way. Yet, somehow, the pair had a long and fruitful marriage. It may be that it worked because they were rarely together, living apart for much of their lives.

With the question of matrimony seemingly settled, though an actual marriage date had not been set, the news of the declaration of war with Mexico on May 12, 1846, riveted Sherman's attention. Not entirely unexpected after Congress had voted to annex Texas, it still offered a young Army officer the prospect of battle, excitement, and perhaps the alluring opportunity to earn military glory. "I am promised to go," Sherman wrote his brother John, "in case this company goes . . . which will inevitably enable me to go to Texas. . . and then most heartily will I give all the aid I can to further the views of Government to extend the 'Area of Freedom.'"

Sherman's prospect of going off to war soon shattered with the arrival of orders sending him to

Pittsburgh, Pennsylvania, on recruiting duty. Even while members of his own regiment mobilized for service in Texas, the ambitious redhead went out of harm's way. One wonders if Thomas Ewing had a hand in this turn of events. It is easy to understand Cump's misery and frustration while he sat idle. "That I should be on recruiting service, when my comrades were actually fighting was intolerable," he lamented. His one consolation: he was close to home and could get to Lancaster often.

Finally, after an interminably long wait, the sullen recruiting officer received orders to hasten to New York for passage to California. His chance had come! So anxious to get to New York, Sherman did not even take the time to visit his mother in nearby Mansfield or Ellen in Lancaster. He folded up shop, packed hurriedly, and penned a short note to his fiancée. "Ordered to California by Sea around Cape Horn, is not this enough to rouse the most placid," Cump wrote disjointedly. He departed "upon a wild and long expedition without any token, any memento save a small lock of hair . . . you will think of me will you not? Farewell Ellen."

Arriving in Monterey, California, in late January 1847, Sherman and his comrades found that after six months at sea, they had arrived too late. The fighting was over—except for squabbles between rival factions who sought to control the territory. Attending to his duty as quartermaster, Cump left others to their disputes and settled into his new responsibilities.

The California adventure was a bust and started one of the gloomiest periods of Sherman's life. Marked by long periods of idleness and boredom, the discovery of gold in the Sacramento Valley offered the only exciting episode of his tenure. However, the subsequent behavior of those with gold fever confirmed his already dim view of human nature. Still, it did provide him with financial opportunity. "Sherman's keenest insight into the gold rush was that a fortune could be made by providing necessities to the prospectors rather than by joining them." This he did with a short-lived store in Coloma, resulting in a tidy $1,500 profit.

Without a doubt, Sherman felt stranded and adrift in California. Thoughts of resigning his commission surfaced from time to time. "I am so completely banished," he wrote Ellen, "that I feel I am losing all hope." When the war with Mexico officially ended in

This adobe building was the quarters of then Lt. William T. Sherman in Monterey, California, in 1847. (WC)

the fall of 1848, Cump knew his opportunity was gone. "I felt deeply," Sherman recalled in his memoirs, "the fact that our country had passed through a foreign war, that my comrades had fought great battles, and yet, I had not heard a hostile shot."

The long California exile ended suddenly and unexpectedly in January 1850 when Sherman traveled on a special mission to deliver a cache of confidential papers to Washington, D. C. Once complete, he looked forward to the promise of extended furlough. Arriving back east, Lt. Sherman's relief mixed once again with a sense of failure when he had the opportunity to dine with General Winfield Scott, conqueror of Mexico City and major hero of the war. With an ego to match his stature, Scott regaled his guests with the exploits of his great Army while Sherman probably gloomily studied his own shoes.

Things brightened on May 1, 1850, when Sherman and Ellen finally married. It had been a long and difficult separation, but the couple survived the experience and were committed to a future together, come what may. The newlyweds enjoyed a fine summer together before Cump's furlough ended in September. New orders arrived with his posting to Jefferson Barracks in St. Louis and a promotion to captain. While the new post and rank delighted Capt. Sherman, Mrs. Sherman was uncertain. She had spent much of the summer trying to convince her husband to give up the Army, to no avail. And, of course, the separation from her parents weighed heavy upon her mind.

For the next several years, the Shermans' life passed pleasantly enough. The newly minted captain returned to St. Louis for a time before being transferred to New Orleans. Life did get more complex and expensive. In January 1851, the first baby joined the ranks. Little Minnie, formally Maria Boyle Ewing, after Ellen's mother, delighted her busy father, who could not wait to begin family life altogether. A second pregnancy soon followed, and Ellen and Minnie returned to Lancaster while Cump traveled on business to Kansas before reporting to his new post in New Orleans. Daughter Mary Elizabeth swelled the ranks in November 1852, and the family now gathered to reside on Magazine Street in New Orleans. It was a busy but generally happy time.

Sherman never imagined returning to California. Briefly, there was the possibility that he would be sent to Oregon, but that did not develop, much to Ellen's relief. However, his return to the West Coast came as a surprise opportunity that seemed to suggest the beginning and end of his military career. "Almost at the moment of [his family's] arrival, also came from St. Louis my personal friend Major Turner, with a parcel of documents," Sherman recalled later, "which on examination, proved to be articles of copartnership for a bank in California . . . in which my name was embraced as a partner." Just days later, James H. Lucas arrived to speak with the eccentric Army

Situated ten miles south of St. Louis on the western bank of the Mississippi River, Jefferson barracks is the oldest operating U.S. military installation west of the Mississippi River. (loc)

LEFT: **Maria "Minnie" Ewing Sherman was the eldest daughter of William Tecumseh Sherman and Eleanor "Ellen" Ewing. In 1874, she married Thomas William Fitch.** (loc)

RIGHT: **Portrait of James H. Lucas in a gilt frame. Painted by J. Reid.** (loc)

captain, with a view to convincing Cump to accept the proposition. "He offered me a very tempting income, with an interest that would accumulate and grow."

Practically blindsided by this sudden turn of events and a bit dazzled by the offer, Sherman, for the first time, considered leaving the Army. He had, of course, declined to do this when Ellen and the Ewings pressed him in this course. The difference now was that an opportunity arrived unbidden and due to his skill and competence. If he accepted the job, it would be because he wanted to do it—not because someone else pressed it upon him. No wonder he felt a bit overwhelmed.

The agreement offered by Lucas, Turner, and Company required Sherman to permanently reside in San Francisco, where he would manage the day-to-day affairs of the bank. Determined to investigate the situation further, before giving up his commission, the prospective banker secured a leave of absence from the Army while he went to California to size up the circumstances. If the opportunity still seemed

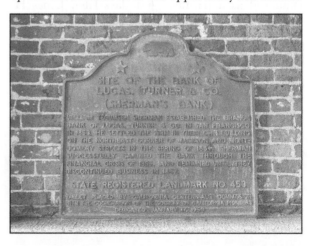

Plaque marking the building that once housed the bank of Lucas & Turner, which was managed by William Tecumseh Sherman. (wc)

Panorama of San Francisco about 1851. (wc)

promising, then he would resign from the Army. This plan delighted Ellen and her family. First, because her husband seriously considered civilian employment—even if it was on the West Coast. Second, it meant the family could return to Lancaster, at least until Cump got settled. The fact that the new position would double the family income pleased everyone.

Nelson A. Miles

WILLIAM T. SHERMAN
General, USA

Concern for learning and regard for experience mark the career of William T. Sherman. Upon his graduation from West Point, he sought service in the Seminole War and later in the war with Mexico. Forced to resign from the army in 1853 because of low pay and increasing family obligations, Sherman undertook a variety of civilian endeavors: banking, practicing law and teaching. He served as the first Superintendent of what would become Louisiana State University.

The secession of Louisiana forced the anguished resignation of General Sherman. He went to St. Louis where he answered the Union's call to arms. His military skills and powers of leadership made his role in Civil War one of ever increasing responsibility - from Shiloh and Vicksburg, through Chattanooga, to Atlanta, and the march through Georgia and South Carolina.

General Sherman became Commanding General of the Army in 1869. He wished to keep alive the fighting spirit of the army in peacetime and to keep it abreast of the latest developments. In order to create an army with sufficient experience to preclude the deadly mistakes of the Civil War, he established the School of Application for Infantry and Cavalry, the forerunner of the Command and General Staff College. General Sherman watched the school closely in its formative years, supervised its organization and curriculum, and instilled in it the sense of soundness and service in the army for which it has become famous.

Service at Fort Leavenworth, 1852

William T. Sherman

In Search of a Calling

CHAPTER THREE

1852–1861

On a harrowing trip to California that included two shipwrecks in 48 hours, the Ohio captain arrived in San Francisco. Determining that the prospects for the bank were good, Cump decided that he would give it a go. After a brief return east, he finalized the agreement with Lucas and Turner and resigned his commission effective September 6, 1853. He then made plans for the whole Sherman brood to travel to California.

After a mostly uneventful journey, the family settled into their new life. The bank prospered, and in 1854, a new building was erected on the corner of Montgomery and Jackson Streets. The climate, however, posed challenges. Sherman's asthma flared during the summer, causing considerable consternation. "I have little or no faith in my prolonged existence," the new banker wrote. Upbraided by his partner Turner for his pessimism, Cump answered, "Why the Devil can't you let an old soldier growl a bit?"

Amidst the snarling, Sherman had reason to celebrate when his first son, William—often called Willie—was born. A redhead like his grumpy father, the boy grew to be a favorite. Later, writing to Ulysses S. Grant, Sherman called Willie "the one I most prised [sic] on earth." Occasionally, Ellen chastised her husband for showing such preference for the boy, but her warnings went unheeded.

Sherman appears in the Hall of Fame at Fort Leavenworth.
(ar)

A view of Montgomery Street in San Francisco where the bank managed by Sherman was located. (wc)

Weathering a banking crisis in 1855, Sherman demonstrated coolness and perseverance. Unlike other banks, Lucas, Turner, and Company survived the challenge. Undoubtedly, the partners had chosen wisely when they tapped Cump to manage their affairs. "He might have chronic doubts about his own abilities and might worry and become depressed," biographer John F. Marszalek wrote of Sherman, "but neither anxiety or depression affected his performance during the run on the bank; he had grown more secure as conditions worsened, acting swiftly, confidently, and efficiently."

An early 20th century view of the old Lucas & Turner Bank building in San Francisco (center). (wc)

Domestic challenges proved more difficult to manage. Incredibly unhappy to be so far from her family, Ellen longed to return to Lancaster. Even after Sherman built her a fine new home, she insisted on returning east with her children. Minnie had been left with her grandparents in Ohio, despite her father's objections, and Ellen eagerly wanted to see her. Not wishing to expose his young children to the perils of travel, Sherman sent his wife off alone to Ohio. She did not return until December 1855.

Despite Sherman's best efforts, the San Francisco branch of Lucas, Turner, and Company bore disappointing profits and had to close. Overjoyed, Ellen wanted to leave immediately. On May 1, 1857, the bank closed its doors, and the Shermans sailed for New York.

While the family returned to Lancaster, Sherman's partners placed him in charge of a bank branch in New York. But the Panic of 1857 spelled an end to his banking career, and he too repaired to Lancaster feeling like an utter failure—the "Jonah of banking."

Down on his luck, the former banker had little choice except to lean on his father-in-law's charity. Cump had studiously avoided this from the beginning, but now he needed the help. So, Sherman ventured off to Leavenworth, Kansas, where his two foster brothers had a law firm. He would work at the law and manage the landholdings of the expanding Ewing empire. Ellen, of course, remained in Lancaster with the children.

While being admitted to the bar counted a success, Sherman did not see it so. In fact, he saw his Kansas interlude as hitting rock bottom. His professional life was a shambles, and his relationship with Ellen was not much better. He thought about returning to the Army. In a letter to his old comrade Don Carlos Buell, now assistant adjutant general of the Army, he pleaded for a post, "anything," Sherman wrote, "in your line that I could obtain." But there was nothing. "However," Buell replied, "I send you a paper which represents an opening that I have been disposed to think well of." Louisiana, as it happened, was looking for a superintendent for its projected military academy. Could that be his ticket out of Kansas? Cump mailed his application with dispatch.

The propitious timing of the Louisiana opportunity brought together both the unhappy Leavenworth lawyer and the Board of Supervisors

Louisiana Governor Robert Wickliffe was elected to office in 1856. In the presidential election of 1860, he supported Sen. Stephen A. Douglas. (pd)

of the new academy. The unimpressed supervisors waded through piles of applications until they found Sherman's. His application cover letter read short and sweet but apparently struck a chord. "I send no testimonials," the eager former soldier wrote, "I will only say that I am a graduate of West Point and an ex-army officer; if you care to know further about me, I refer you to the officers of the army from General Scott down, and in your own state to Col. Braxton Bragg, Major G. T. Beauregard and Richard Taylor, Esq."

Confident that he had an excellent chance of being hired for the job in Louisiana, Sherman wasted little time. "I closed up my business at Leavenworth, and went to Lancaster, Ohio," he recalled later, "where, in July, 1859, I received notice from Governor Wickliffe that I had been elected superintendent of the proposed college, and inviting me to come down to Louisiana as early as possible." News of his appointment did not sit well with the Ewings, who had wanted him to go to London to pursue another banking job. This mattered little to the new professor, who anxiously wanted to escape a position entirely within the Ewing orbit. "I am going to take the bit in my mouth, and resume my military character, and control my own affairs," he told Ellen.

That Louisiana built a military academy while a potential war loomed troubled Sherman. He understood that the institution of slavery steered the country towards a dangerous split. While he was not a fan of slavery, neither did he advocate for its abolition. He saw abolitionists as troublemakers, unnecessarily stirring up passions. To his brother John, now a member of Congress, he counseled moderation. "As you are becoming a man of note and are a Republican, and as I go South among gentlemen who have always owned slaves, and probably always will and must, and whose feelings may pervert every public expression of yours . . . I would like to see you take the highest ground consistent with your party creed."

Sherman arrived in Alexandria, Louisiana— the site of the academy—in late summer of 1859 and set to work with a will. With the assistance of George Mason Graham, president of the Board of Supervisors, a whirlwind of activity led to the hoped-for opening in January 1860. Equipment was acquired, uniforms designed and ordered, and other academies consulted—including the Virginia

Military Institute and West Point—about policy and procedures. Nothing escaped Cump's attention, and he worked tirelessly to be ready for the first class to arrive.

Styled the Louisiana Seminary of Learning and Military Academy, the institution opened its doors to the first cadets in early January. However, it missed the projected target of students by half. Hoping for one hundred, only fifty-one rallied by late January. A slow start, but the school had opened and was operating.

Situated on a hill not far from the village of Alexandria, the academy sat on about four hundred acres. The main building rose three stories, comprising more than thirty rooms, and boasted five towers that added some flair to the otherwise institutional-looking structure. The superintendent began his tenure as a resident of one of the rooms of the seminary to be on-the-spot as things got underway.

As he had expected, Sherman's relation to John became known and drew attention. One evening at a dinner, Governor Moore and a large group of prominent men, including many state legislators, called out Sherman's brother and beliefs. "Colonel Sherman . . . with your brother the abolitionist candidate for Speaker, some of our people wonder that you should be here at the head of an important State institution," the governor exclaimed. "Now, you are at my table, and I assure you of my confidence. Won't you speak your mind freely on this question of slavery, that so agitates the land?"

Never at a loss for words and prepared as he had been for something of this kind, Sherman first boldly

Thomas Overton Moore was governor of Louisiana during the Civil War. A champion of education, Moore had led the effort to create the Louisiana Seminary of Learning and Military Academy. (loc)

Louisiana State Seminary of Learning and Military Academy was located in Pineville, Louisiana. The first building, pictured, was completed in 1859. (loc)

Ruins of the original building at the site of the Louisiana Seminary of Learning and Military Academy in Pineville, Louisiana. After the war, the school was moved to Baton Rouge. (wc)

defended his brother. "Governor Moore, you mistake in calling my brother, John Sherman, an abolitionist." True, the congressman preferred free labor, but "he would not of himself take from you by law or force any property whatever, even slaves." The superintendent went on to make it clear that he was not in favor of the abolition of slavery but would "were I a citizen of Louisiana, and a member of the Legislature" make some changes. First, he would "forbid the separation of families, letting the father, mother, and children, be sold together to one person." He also advocated for "repeal of the statute" that imposed harsh penalties on those who taught slaves to read and write, arguing that it was counterproductive. Those skills would increase the value of the slaves, illustrating the point with an example from his tenure in California. Sherman's performance at dinner apparently satisfied the curiosity of the folks present. In any case, it did no harm to his position or influence.

The end of the first term at the seminary occurred in July 1860 and was celebrated with a ball. A long recess followed, and everyone departed to their homes—students, faculty, and some staff—not to return until November. Sherman kept busy, traveling to Washington, New York, and finally Lancaster to see his family. Though he returned to Louisiana, his family remained in Ohio for now.

The new term at the seminary began on schedule in November with 130 cadets—some returning, others new to the academy. By now, a new house had been prepared for Sherman and his family, but he moved in alone. "I had moved into my new house," the superintendent wrote, "but prudently had not sent for my family, nominally on the ground of waiting until the season was further advanced, but really because of the storm that was lowering heavy on the political horizon." The presidential election riveted the attention of the nation.

The presidential election of 1860 loomed momentously, filled with the possibility of causing disunion. The Republicans nominated Abraham Lincoln of Illinois, and the Democratic Party split. John Breckinridge ran on the Southern Democratic ticket, and Stephen Douglas was the nominee of the Democratic Party. The Constitutional Union Party nominated John Bell. The election seemed like a recipe for trouble. First, because of all the presidential candidates, it was a real possibility that no one would receive the majority of the electoral votes necessary for victory, which would mean that the House of Representatives would then elect the president. Also, many Southern states made it clear that if Lincoln won, disunion would immediately follow.

John Cabell Breckinridge was a Kentucky politician who became the youngest vice president of the United States in 1857 at just 36. (loc)

Sherman found himself in a delicate position. "I purposely kept aloof from politics," he said in his memoirs. He had been left alone and not been pressured until election day, "when I was notified that it would be advisable for me to vote for Bell and Everett, but I openly said that I would not, and I did not." When the results became known, "The election of Mr. Lincoln fell upon us all like a clap of thunder." Sherman watched and waited. He expected the worst but still hoped for the best.

"Well, Lincoln is elected," Sherman wrote his brother John in late November 1860. Now all eyes turned to South Carolina. "It is evident we have to meet in serious form the movements of South Carolinian Disunionists. These men for years have desired this disunion; they have plotted for it." Instead of waiting for passions to cool, the hot heads rushed into secession. How would the other slave states react? "Secession is revolution," Sherman declared.

While the term at the academy advanced more or less normally, the superintendent knew that he would face critical decisions soon. "I know we will have trouble this winter," he wrote, but whatever happens, "I will insist on preserving the unity of the States, and all the States without exception and without regard to consequences." He would have to take his stand soon since the Louisiana legislature was sure to call for a convention. "When the convention meets in January," Sherman wrote forebodingly, "and resolve to secede. . . . I must quit this place."

Sen. Stephen Douglas of Illinois was nicknamed the Little Giant. (loc)

A former Speaker of the House of Representatives and Secretary of War, John Bell was a candidate for president in the election of 1860 for the Constitutional Union Party. (loc)

Sherman was dining with Professor Boyd when news arrived that South Carolina had seceded. "Sherman began pacing the floor, tears falling, his tongue flinging despair," Boyd recalled. The transplanted Ohioan turned to his friend and lashed out:

You, you the people of the South, believe there can be such a thing as peaceable secession. You don't know what you are doing. I know there can be no such thing. . . . If you will have it, the North must fight you for its own preservation. Yes, South Carolina has by this act precipitated war. . . . This country will be drenched in blood. . . . Oh, it is all folly, madness, a crime against civilization.

Sherman saw that he would have to leave Louisiana and go North. But to what? Once again, he would be adrift. War seemed inevitable.

You people speak so lightly of war. You don't know what you are talking about. War is a terrible thing. . . . You mistake, too, the people of the North. They are a peaceable people, but an earnest people and will fight too, and they are not going to let this country be destroyed without a mighty effort to save it . . . [Y]ou are bound to fail. Only in your spirit and determination are you prepared for war. In all else you are totally unprepared, with a bad cause to start with.

Awaiting the secession of Louisiana amounted to torture for Sherman as he sat powerless to alter the course of the state. He pondered his next move. Before the Louisiana convention met, Governor Moore ordered the seizure of the U.S. arsenal at Baton Rouge. Some of those seized arms headed to the military seminary for deposit, and the superintendent would then have to accept them and provide a receipt. This Sherman refused to do. His resignation quickly followed.

President-elect Abraham Lincoln. On his way to Washington, DC, for his inauguration, Lincoln had to be smuggled through Baltimore secretly to assure his security. (loc)

Sir:

As I occupy a quasi-military position under the laws of the State, I deem it proper to acquaint you that I accepted such a position when Louisiana was a State in the Union and when the motto of this Seminary was inserted in marble over the main door: "By the liberality of the general government of the United States. The Union—esto perpetua."

Recent events foreshadow a great change and it becomes all men to choose. If Louisiana withdraw from the Federal Union, I prefer to maintain my allegiance to the constitution as long as a fragment of it survives and my longer stay here would be wrong in every sense of the word.

In that event I beg you will send or appoint some authorized agent to take charge of the arms and munitions of war belonging to the state or advise me what disposition to make of them.

And furthermore, as president of the Board of Supervisors, I beg you to take immediate steps to relieve me as superintendent the moment the state determines to secede, for on no earthly account will I do any act or think any thought hostile or in defiance to the old government of the United States.

W. T. Sherman
Superintendent

The pro-secession *Mercury* was founded in 1819 and had a long history—but would cease publication permanently soon after the Civil War. (wc)

Once his affairs were in order, the redheaded loner turned north, again unemployed. He pleaded with John to find him a job in the Treasury Department. His old partner Turner offered to find a place for him in St. Louis. Thomas Ewing spoke about a position overseeing the Salt Works. He had some choices.

When the superintendent said goodbye, according to biographer Lloyd Lewis, "The boys wept, the superintendent wept. Sherman finally managed to say that he couldn't make the speech he had intended; he "put his hand on his heart, saying, 'you are all here,' wheeled on his heel and was gone." Once his affairs were in order to the satisfaction of the Board of Supervisors, Sherman boarded a steamboat for passage up the Mississippi and then on to Lancaster.

David French Boyd was one of the original professors at the Louisiana State Seminary of Learning and Military Academy. During the war, he joined the Confederate Army. (pd)

War Beckons

CHAPTER FOUR

1861

Dejected by the premature end to his academy career, the former superintendent made his way home via river and rail. Along the way, he noted with interest, "In the South, the people were earnest, fierce, and angry, and were evidently organizing for action," Sherman recalled later. "Whereas, in Illinois, Indiana, and Ohio, I saw not the least sign of preparation. It certainly looked to me as though the people of the North would tamely submit to a disruption of the Union." Perhaps there would be no war.

Arriving home in early March 1861, Sherman must have felt disoriented and pulled in every direction. Now, his family wanted him in the army. His friend Turner argued for a return to St. Louis, where he wanted to make the former banker into the president of the railroad his firm operated. His brother John, elevated to the U.S. Senate, had a newfound influence that promised opportunity if he would only go to Washington, D.C. Hedging his bets, Sherman gladly accepted the St. Louis job and packed his bags for the capital.

Senator Sherman wasted little time finding a place for his gloomy brother. With easy access to the halls of power, the pair headed straight to the White House, where they marched directly to the president's office and gained entry. "Mr. President, this is my brother, Colonel Sherman," John said to Lincoln, "he may give you some information you want." "Ah," Lincoln responded, "how are they getting along down there?"

Looking down the barrel of a gun at Manassas National Battlefield Park in Virginia. Site of two important Civil War battles, the area was first protected by the Federal government in 1940. (ddm)

Prior to his tenure as president of the Confederate States of America, Jefferson Davis had been a distinguished secretary of war in President Franklin Pierce's cabinet. (loc)

"They think they are getting along swimmingly—they are preparing for war," Sherman answered. "Oh, well!" the Commander-in-Chief lamely replied, "I guess we'll manage to keep house." That, apparently, was not the answer Cump hoped for. Shocked into silence, Sherman said little until alone with John. "You have got things in a hell of a fix, and you may get them out as you best can," Sherman burst out.

Lincoln and Sherman first met each other at a bad moment. Office seekers besieged the president, making him feel overwhelmed, and the redhead was mad at the world. Senator Sherman begged his brother to be patient, but reason did not get very far with him. The elder brother stomped off to St. Louis, and the politicians be damned.

Amid Sherman's months-long pout, the war started in earnest when President Lincoln attempted to resupply Fort Sumter in Charleston Harbor, South Carolina. There, Cump's old friend, Maj. Robert Anderson holed up after removing his command from Fort Moultrie. Without more provisions, Anderson would be forced to surrender his men. Lincoln knew the effort to resupply the fort might bring on war, but to his mind, at least he would not be the aggressor. He even gave the governor of South Carolina advance notice.

On orders from Jefferson Davis, provisional president of the Confederate States of America, one of Sherman's other old friends, P. G. T. Beauregard, gave the order to fire on Fort Sumter in the early morning of April 12, 1861. Anderson held out awhile to satisfy honor but then surrendered his command. Lincoln responded by calling for 75,000 volunteers for three months of service. There was no mistake; the Civil War had been inaugurated.

Even then, with the North in turmoil, Sherman declined offer after offer. The War Department dangled a clerkship, Frank Blair of the famous politically powerful Blair clan proposed a brigadier generalship. Cump's family could not understand his intransigence. He turned down a general's star? What was he thinking? "The time will come in this country when professional knowledge will be appreciated," Sherman explained, "when men that can be trusted will be wanted, and I will bide my time. I may miss the chance; if so alright; but I cannot and will not mix myself in the present call."

A graduate of the U.S. Military Academy at West Point, Pierre Gustave Toutant-Beauregard briefly served as its superintendent on the eve of the Civil War. (loc)

Sherman did not miss the chance. It came quickly, and he snapped at the opportunity. A telegram from John announced that he had been made colonel of the 13th U.S. Regular Infantry but that he had to take command immediately. This meant a place in the regular army with permanent rank. He would command regulars, not volunteers. The job checked all the boxes, and the wiry new colonel left for Washington without delay.

The situation in the capital devolved into a confused mess. Arriving before his regiment had even been recruited, Sherman joined General Winfield Scott's staff, inspecting troops around Washington. Then in early summer, word came about a planned advance against two Confederate armies in Virginia. Brigadier General Irvin McDowell would lead the offensive since Scott, at age 75, was too old to take the field. Colonel Sherman took command of a brigade in the First Division.

On July 15, the Union army of 35,000 lurched in motion on its way to Manassas Junction, where Confederate General P. G. T. Beauregard, Sherman's old friend, waited with about 22,000 troops. Out in the Shenandoah Valley, General Joseph E. Johnston had about 7,000 more. Union General Robert Patterson, with 16,000 men, had the task of keeping Johnston's

When the order came to fire on Ft. Sumter, Virginia Congressman Roger Pryor was offered the chance to fire the first shot. He declined. (loc)

Maj. Gen. Frank Blair was from the powerful Blair family, whose motto was said to be "When the Blairs go in for a fight, they go in for a funeral." (loc)

After graduating from West Point in 1838, Irvin McDowell taught infantry tactics there from 1841–1845. (loc)

The first battle of Bull Run, fought July 21, 1861, was a Confederate victory. Brig. Gen. Irvin McDowell commanded the Union Army of Northeastern Virginia. (loc)

men penned up and unable to reinforce Beauregard. In this, Patterson utterly failed.

The battle of First Bull Run, also known as the battle of First Manassas, erupted on July 21, 1861. McDowell, with an army of green volunteers, designed an intricate flank attack that nearly worked. But it all began to unravel as the Union pushed the Rebels up Henry House Hill, where they stalled, largely due to the stoic stubbornness of Confederate General Thomas "Stonewall" Jackson. A counterattack from fresh Confederate troops scattered Union regiments, who fell back reluctantly with some order. However, a panic seized the Union ranks, and the retreat turned into a rout.

Despite two minor wounds and his horse shot out from under him, Sherman performed well and brought his men off the field in good order. Thinking back on the experience, the eccentric Ohioan wrote, "We had good organization, good men, but no cohesion, no real discipline, no respect for authority, no real knowledge of war." Still mortified, he concluded, "It is now generally admitted that it was one of the best planned battles of the war, but one of the worst fought."

"Well as I am sufficiently disgraced now," Sherman wrote to Ellen a few days after his return to Washington. "I suppose soon I can sneak into some

BATTLE OF BULL RUN.

The home of Judith Henry, Henry House, sat on the field where the battle of Bull Run occurred. Widow Henry was 84 and bedridden at the time of the battle. (loc)

quiet corner." Detailing the battle and its aftermath for her, the dejected colonel said, "I had read of retreats before—have seen the noise and confusion of crowds of men at fires and shipwrecks but nothing like this." He did not know what the future held in store, but his faith was wavering. "Our rulers think more of who shall get office, than who can save the country. Nobody—no one man can save the country. The difficulty is with the masses—our men are not good soldiers—they brag, but don't perform—complain sadly if they don't get everything they want—and a march of a few miles uses them up."

Like many others in Washington and in the army, Sherman recovered slowly from the defeat at Bull Run. However, the humiliation did not lead to a failure of will, but rather bolstered the desire to do better next time. Confederate officials had hoped that the Union disaster would spell an end to the war; their soaring confidence meant they were ready and even eager to continue the fight.

Promotion to brigadier general in August did little to boost Sherman's confidence or morale. According to historian Charles Edmund Vetter, "He did not want to fail again; thus he became extremely cautious and calculating." Then, that same month, an unexpected offer promised a change of circumstances. Robert Anderson, the hero of Fort Sumter and now a major general, reached out to his former Fort Moultrie comrade. He wanted Sherman to be his second in command when he took over the new Department of the Cumberland to provide support to Unionists in Kentucky and Tennessee.

Happy to assist his old friend and get out of Washington, Sherman accepted. The situation in Kentucky especially was delicate. Though the

Lt. Gen. Thomas J. Jackson was a dedicated Confederate officer, but his sister Laura Jackson Arnold was a fervent Unionist who became estranged from her brother. (loc)

Nicknamed "The Pathfinder," John C. Fremont was a pompous loner who once attended Charleston College in South Carolina. In 1831, he was expelled for irregular attendance. (loc)

Maj. Gen. John C. Fremont's headquarters sat at Eighth Street and Chouteau Avenue in St. Louis when he commanded the Department of the West during the Civil War. Fremont was said to have a bodyguard of 150 men. (wc)

birthplace of Lincoln, the bluegrass state abounded with Confederate sentiment. The slave state also declared neutrality, initially refusing to join either side. Anderson anxiously approached the situation and actually made his headquarters in Cincinnati, waiting for the right moment to enter the Bluegrass State.

Uncertain prospects loomed for securing Kentucky for the Union, but the means to support Kentucky looked worse. "Here we have no means of offense, and but little of defense," Sherman told his brother, "And if you are full of zeal, you could not do better than to raise your voice to call the young and middle-aged men of Ohio to arms." Convinced that a Confederate thrust into Kentucky was in the making, Anderson and Sherman reached out in all directions for men and arms but met with little success.

The mid-western states had already worked on their response to Maj. Gen. John C. Fremont's call for troops as he gathered an army from his headquarters in St. Louis. Sherman begged the Pathfinder—as he had been dubbed in his days of exploring the West— for men to defend Kentucky. A trip to St. Louis might have had the added benefit of calming Sherman's jangled nerves.

Fremont and Sherman were not the best of friends, but they had been acquainted in California. The new brigadier was unprepared, however, for the reception he got at Fremont's headquarters. Arriving in the early morning, Sherman encountered "a sentinel with drawn saber [who] paraded up and down in front of the house." Gaining admittance proved to be a chore,

Residence & Head Quarters of Gen'l Fremont in St. Louis

despite the star on his shoulders. Finally, "the main front-door above was slowly opened from the inside," the impatient redhead recalled, "and who should appear but my old San Francisco acquaintance Isaiah C. Woods." Now on Fremont's staff, Woods helped secure an audience with the pretentious Pathfinder.

The environs of the meeting with Fremont gained more notice than any productive results. While he promised Sherman cooperation, the pompous general mostly wanted to pick Cump's brain for opinions on artillery, citizens of St. Louis, and matters unrelated to Kentucky. Irked by Fremont's fortress headquarters and unnecessary pomp, Sherman worried about evidence of corruption that would later bring about the Pathfinder's downfall. "The result I have come to is that [Fremont] has called about him men who will swindle the government and bring disgrace on us all," Sherman wrote Ellen. "I could not discover that he was operating on any distinct plan . . . [but] by proclamations and threats which there is no power to execute he has completed what Lyons began in alienating the support of all the moderate men of the city."

With headquarters now in Louisville and Kentucky leaning firmly in the Union column—despite many Kentucky youth who joined the ranks of the Confederate army—Sherman worked long days to try to meet the other dangers he saw lurking. "The Confederates kept moving and feinting and marching . . . and they convinced Sherman and the other Unionists that there were more than enough of them to crush the minuscule Federal units in Kentucky." Meanwhile, the overall Confederate commander in the center, General Albert Sidney Johnston—a favorite of Jefferson Davis—"complained that he had not gunpowder for any campaign." If only Sherman had known.

To the cynical Sherman, matters looked dark indeed. Then disaster struck; Anderson resigned on October 8th under pressure, and now the volatile redhead had no choice except to assume command. In truth, the fifty-six-year-old Anderson was not up to the job from the beginning. Various maladies plagued him, and the stress of the situation wore him down.

Department command was the last thing Sherman wanted at this stage of his career. He did not feel equal to the occasion. Evidence of the new commander's concern is found in a telegram he sent directly to the

Confederate Gen. Albert Sidney Johnston once served as the Secretary of War in the Republic of Texas. (loc)

Secretary of War Simon Cameron was a former U.S. Senator from Pennsylvania. Said to be thoroughly corrupt, Lincoln dismissed Cameron and appointed him the U.S. Minister to Russia. (loc)

White House, bypassing the chain of command. "My own belief is that Confederates will make a more desperate effort to join Kentucky than they have for Missouri. Force now here or expected is entirely inadequate," the brigadier told the Commander-in-Chief. "All men in Ind. and Ohio are ready to come to Ky. But they have no arms and we cannot supply them arms clothing or anything." As if to push the limits of subordination, Sherman concluded curtly, "Answer."

When Secretary of War Simon Cameron passed through the area on his way to investigate Fremont's machinations, Sherman took the opportunity to press his case. He needed to make an impression on the secretary here and now. Troop levies from the Midwest continued to be funneled to other commands, leaving his department vulnerable. "If [General Albert Sidney] Johnston chose, he could march to Louisville any day," Sherman asserted. Taken aback, Cameron responded that he had been assured by the Kentucky Senators that there were plenty of men available, just not adequate arms. Cump told the secretary this was not the case, and Cameron assured him that help would be on the way.

To help illustrate not only his needs, but the long view of the resources necessary in the West, Sherman then pulled out a large map. He had over three hundred burdensome miles of front to defend with less than 20,000 men; McClellan, who had 100,000, defended less than one hundred miles of front in the east. As Sherman wrote in his memoir, "I argued that, for the purpose of defense, we should have sixty thousand men at once, and for offense, we need two hundred thousand, before we were done." Slack-jawed, Cameron answered, "Great God! Where are they to come from?"

Satisfied that his meeting with Cameron had impressed the gravity of the situation in Kentucky, Sherman had, in fact, overdone it. The overly dramatic—indeed shocking—assertions only served to inspire wonder in those present, including several reporters unbeknownst to Sherman, as to the mental soundness of the general. Later, in a letter to the adjutant general, Sherman lamented, "It would be better if some more sanguine mind were here."

In early November, Sherman found in the New York Tribune, dated October 30, a very unflattering account of his meeting with Cameron contained in Adjutant General Lorenzo Thomas's official report.

Omitting Sherman's request for 60,000 men for defense, the report focused instead on "Sherman's estimate of 200,000 troops for offensive operations [which] was cast in an absurd vein." Angry, the Ohio-born general fired off a retort to Thomas. "Do not conclude," he wrote, "that I exaggerate the facts. They are as stated, and the future looks as dark as possible." This, of course, did not help Sherman's case.

Finally, on November 8, Sherman asked to be relieved. Biding his time until Brig. Gen. Don Carlos Buell replaced him a few weeks later; the grizzled warrior seemed to recognize the overwhelming situation and perhaps a need for rest. Reflecting on this in his memoirs, he later wrote that he felt "the manifest belief that there was more or less of truth in the rumor that the care, perplexities, and anxiety of the situation had unbalanced my judgement."

A regular army officer from Delaware, Lorenzo Thomas was adjutant general of the U.S. Army during the Civil War. (loc)

Ordered to report in person to Maj. Gen. Henry "Old Brains" Halleck for duty in St. Louis, Sherman might have felt relief from being unburdened of command. However, the easy duty inspecting troops proved to be anything except tranquil. "But the newspapers kept harping on my insanity and paralyzed my efforts," Sherman recalled later. Frustrated, he lashed out. "In spite of myself, they tortured from me some words and acts of impudence." Then, in late November, Sherman received a message from headquarters that began, "Mrs. Sherman is here." He was being sent home.

Halleck had seen enough. "I am satisfied that General S[herman]'s physical and mental system is so completely broken by labor and care as to render him for the present entirely unfit for duty." McClellan was notified. "Perhaps a few weeks rest will restore him." Quite the eccentric himself, "Old Brains" famously played both sides of the street. To the Ewings, Halleck offered all sympathy and showed sincere concern for Cump's health and well-being. To McClellan, now General-in-Chief, Halleck wrote, "It would be dangerous to give him a command here."

Back in Lancaster, just as Sherman showed signs of recovery, the headline "General William T. Sherman Insane" appeared in the Cincinnati Commercial. The allegations presented in support of the headline included frequent unhinged appeals to Washington, overestimating the strength of the enemy, giving up Cumberland Gap, and issuing orders so incredulous

Maj. Gen. Henry Halleck was appointed general in chief of Union armies during the war. His performance in this capacity disappointed President Lincoln, who said Halleck was little better than "a first-rate clerk." (loc)

Maj. Gen. George B. McClellan served briefly as the commanding general of Union armies, but was demoted in the spring of 1862. He ran afoul of Lincoln, who relieved him for good after the battle of Antietam. (loc)

that subordinates refused to comply. He was, in their words, "stark mad."

Other newspapers soon piled on, exacting revenge for Sherman's past treatment of their journalist brethren. It had been no secret that the general despised newspaper correspondents. From time to time, he had high-handedly admonished or even expelled them from camp. Even back in his California days, reporters had been his nemesis. With blood in the water, the correspondents responded like sharks.

Down, but not quite out, the Ewing family "cavalry" charged to the rescue. All the strength and political power of the family now mustered to retrieve the battered reputation of their adopted kin. Thomas Ewing, Philemon, and Ellen and Sherman's Senator brother, John, all used, through various methods, to fight off the scurrilous charges. Some considered lawsuits while John threatened a congressional investigation, and others prayed. For his part, Sherman just wanted to keep his head down and get back to work.

Halleck welcomed him back at the end of his leave, anxious to curry favor with the powerful Ewing/Sherman clan. "Old Brains" found an unobtrusive place supervising Benton Barracks near St. Louis, where he could place and keep a close eye on his old friend Cump. While he found the post beneath him, Sherman appreciated the need to slowly regain the trust and confidence of the people around him.

Historians have long wondered what happened to Sherman in Kentucky. Surely, when measured against later events, the high-strung redhead was not insane. Depression and anxiety seem likely. In his biography, *The Scourge of War: The Life of William Tecumseh Sherman*, historian Brian Holden Reid offers a fresh take on the controversy. Disclaiming Post-Traumatic Stress Disorder (PTSD), which "is a chronic, relapsing disorder," Reid concludes it would have prevented the general's later great success. Instead, Reid suggests adjustment disorder.

Adjustment disorder is a condition that occurs when subjective distress and emotional disturbance interfere with social functioning and performance. This arises during the period of adaptation to significant events beyond an individual's control. Such an experience uproots a life and introduces great levels of stress.

While diagnosing Sherman's malady more than 160 years after the fact is problematic, Reid's perceptive suggestion is serious food for thought. Since adjustment disorder is temporary and patients often have rapid recoveries, there does seem to be a convincing case to be made. Like Lincoln, Sherman exhibited melancholia in episodes throughout this life, but the Kentucky affair never recurred. Time, success, and confidence seemed to be the cure.

A training facility for new recruits during the Civil War, Benton Barracks was located at the site of the St. Louis Fairgrounds. (loc)

A Star Is Born

CHAPTER FIVE
JANUARY–JULY 1862

The rehabilitating assignment to Benton Barracks undoubtedly gave Sherman time to get his feet on the ground and clear his head. Moreover, he produced immediate results, which gratified Halleck. Edging cautiously toward offensive operations, "Old Brains" needed field commanders. "When it does come there is no one who I had rather have with me than yourself," Halleck wrote his subordinate.

Meanwhile, in February 1862, General Ulysses S. Grant's capture of Fort Henry on the Tennessee River with considerable Federal naval support marked an important turning point in Sherman's fortunes. Reflecting his closeness to Halleck at this stage of the war, the barracks commander wrote, "I have always given Halleck the full credit for that movement, which was skillful, successful, and extremely rich in military results; indeed, it was the first real success on our side in the Civil War."

Grant wasted little time and immediately marched a force overland to lay siege to Fort Donelson on the Cumberland River. Wishing to push the movement, though Grant's aggressiveness disconcerted Halleck's cautious nature, "Old Brains" sent Sherman new orders, assigning him to command at Paducah, Kentucky. Here, Sherman would support Grant's campaign by forwarding men and supplies. General Strong would take command of Benton Barracks. This inched the anxious redhead closer to a field command, and he responded with enthusiasm.

The battle of Shiloh gets its name from a small wooden church on the battlefield near Sherman's position. Sherman himself was not a religious man. (cm)

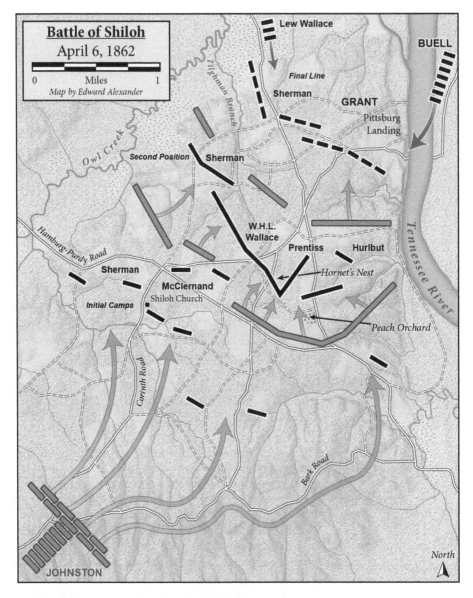

BATTLE OF SHILOH—The battle of Shiloh turned Sherman's life around and did much to rehabilitate his reputation. Fought April 6–7, 1862, the battle was the first big battle of the war and signaled to both sides that the war would neither be short nor bloodless.

The job at Paducah proved to be a good fit for Sherman. A former quartermaster, the eccentric brigadier "had a sure grasp of the important factors of supply and transport," Vetter asserts, "and he used them well. Grant surely thought so. In his memoirs, the conqueror of Fort Donelson wrote,

During the siege General Sherman had been sent to Smithland, at the mouth of the Cumberland River, to forward reinforcements and supplies to me. At that time, he was my senior in rank and there was no authority of law to assign a junior to command a senior of the same grade. But every boat that came up with supplies or reinforcements brought a note of encouragement from Sherman, asking me to call upon him for any assistance he could render and saying that if he could be of service at the front, I might send for him and he would waive rank.

The capture of Forts Henry and Donelson electrified the country and vaulted Grant into the history books. Though Halleck should have been pleased with the brilliant campaign as senior commander and Grant's superior, the success only riled him with jealousy, even though he had also received credit for the victory. Sherman, still at Paducah, wrote to Senator Sherman: "Grant's victory was most extraordinary and brilliant—he was a plain unostentatious man, and a few years ago was of bad habits, but he certainly has done a brilliant act." Not well acquainted just yet, Sherman now had his eye on his fellow Ohioan and took careful note of him. Still, his opinion of Halleck at this point was higher: "I have the most unlimited confidence in Halleck—he is the ablest man by far that as thus far appeared."

Born Hiram Ulysses Grant in Point Pleasant, Ohio, Grant was raised in a Methodist family, though he never attended church. Years later, his son suggested that his father was probably agnostic. (loc)

Print by Kurz and Allison (1887) depicting the battle of Fort Donelson in February 1862. (loc)

Located on the Cumberland River, the Confederate Fort Donelson laid near the town of Dover, Tennessee. Today the battlefield is preserved and operated by the National Parks Service. (loc)

Sherman felt ready to take the field. His self-confidence improved, though his outlook on the war changed little. "The war is not yet over," he wrote to brother John. "I mistrust the Union sentiment now so much spoken of—I hear of it but can't find it." Finally, on March 10, Sherman received orders to take command of a division and to report to General C. F. Smith at Fort Henry, Grant having been temporarily relieved of command due to Halleck's pettiness. Smith ordered Sherman to embark with his division and prepare to cut the Memphis and Charleston railroad.

A torrential downpour caused the Tennessee River to rise by 15 feet and doomed Sherman's first mission with his new division. The sopping brigadier returned to Savannah, seeking new orders and dejected by failing his first assignment. He found General Smith on his deathbed, suffering from an infection caused by an abrasion. Sherman was ordered to take command of General Hurlbut's division, keeping his own at Pittsburg Landing—an old steamboat landing, seemingly in the middle of nowhere, but with roads leading south through a wilderness to Corinth, Mississippi.

At this point, Sherman suggested a raid against the Memphis and Charleston Railroad while simultaneously feinting against Corinth, a major railroad hub. There, it was believed that Confederate General Albert Sidney Johnston had an army of 30,000. With Smith's approval, the plan's action began, using an irregular collection of cavalry. The resulting hour-long cavalry skirmish demonstrated that Confederates already watched Union forces closely and were on high alert to attempted forays. Sherman stewed, frustrated in his efforts to reach the railroad. Then word arrived that Grant had returned to command the Army of the Tennessee and would arrive soon.

There had been some changes in the Union military organization in the West. Halleck had been elevated to overall command, whereas he had been just a departmental commander—the equal of General Buell. Now, Buell was under his command, commanding the Army of the Ohio. Immensely ambitious, Halleck anxiously looked for more success and perhaps another promotion that would land him in Washington. Grant had been instructed to wait and make a junction with Buell's army in readiness for a push south, perhaps against Corinth.

Sherman felt secure as his division camped near a little log church called Shiloh. "The position was naturally strong," he recalled, "with Snake Creek on our right, a deep, bold stream, with a confluence (Owl Creek) to our right front; and Lick Creek . . . on our left." Still, in early April he and his subordinate commanders detected an uptick in Rebel activity to

Maj. Gen. Charles Ferguson Smith was Commandant of Cadets at the U.S. Military Academy at West Point from 1838–1843. His most famous cadet was Ulysses S. Grant, who graduated in 1843. (loc)

Print depicting the original log church that sat inland from Pittsburg Landing, Tennessee. The church was destroyed during the battle of Shiloh but reconstructed in 2003. (loc)

The reconstructed Shiloh Church at the Shiloh National Military Park was built by the Tennessee Sons of Confederate Veterans. (ddm)

The battle of Shiloh was also known as the battle of Pittsburg Landing. Casualties on both sides exceeded 23,700, which made it the bloodiest battle of the Civil War to that date. (loc)

their front. On April 4, Confederate cavalry picked off a company of pickets. Something was up.

Unknown to Sherman and Grant, Albert Sidney Johnston was planning to hit them at Pittsburg Landing before Buell could arrive. The Confederate army had lurched into motion on April 3 in an ill-coordinated, stop-and-go march of just over 20 miles. By the evening of April 5, the blue and gray armies lay close to one another. Yet, Union forces seemingly expected nothing. "The enemy is saucy," Sherman wrote Grant, but "I do not apprehend anything like an attack on our position."

By the dawn of the 6th, Union skirmishers exchanged fire with the lead elements of Johnston's

army. Sherman got his first look at Rebel infantry a few hours later when he saw "the glistening bayonets of heavy masses of infantry to our left front in the woods . . . and became satisfied for the first time that the enemy designed a determined attack on our whole camp." Sherman quickly organized a defensive line, sending word to neighboring commanders. Soon, flying lead filled the air. Many troops fled, including some of Sherman's men.

By the time Grant arrived, hours later, the Union position had pulled back. Marszalek described the situation, "Prentiss retreated until he came to an old road, sufficiently sunken to give him some protection from attackers, and then took a stand." The Union's right line included Sherman, William Wallace, and McClernand. Hurlbut was positioned on Prentiss's left. Grant had sent for Lew Wallace, whose troops waited at Crumps Landing. Buell had not yet arrived with his army.

Maj. Gen. Lew Wallace was a Union officer that participated in the battles of Fort Donelson, Shiloh, and Monocacy. After the war, he served as governor of the New Mexico territory and in 1881 was appointed U.S. Minister to the Ottoman Empire. (loc)

The din of battle was deafening. Met by determined and repeated attacks with heavy artillery fire, Sherman had little choice except to give up his camps and pull back. By 11:00 A.M., he had lost eight guns—five of them lost when the teamsters panicked and fled. Despite a painful wound to the hand, the Ohioan remained "cool, calculating, forthright and decisive." Despite the occasional panicked flight by groups of his men, Sherman largely kept his command intact and well in hand. Three horses had been shot out from under him, a spent ball had badly bruised his shoulder, his hand dripped blood, and an orderly had been killed at his side, but through it all, he remained calm and in control.

Buell's army arrived opposite Pittsburg Landing about 1:00 P.M. A few hours later, they entered the fight and passed through a mass of disconsolate men, huddling under the bluff and seeking shelter from the deluge of metal. Once again, Sherman pulled back to protect a bridge over Owl Creek. With his share in the battle largely over, the pugnacious redhead wondered if Grant would retreat under the cover of night.

Bundled against heavy rain, Sherman found Grant near the landing under a large tree, puffing industriously on a cigar. We've had the "devil's own day," the lanky brigadier told his commander. "Yes," Grant commented dryly, "lick 'em tomorrow though." They would stay and fight it out. After all, Buell's army had arrived fresh and was already crossing the river.

Union Maj. Gen. Benjamin Mayberry Prentiss was born in Virginia and was an auctioneer and rope-maker as a young man. (loc)

At the end of the first day's battle at Pittsburg Landing, Generals Sherman and Grant met in a pouring rain and plotted what the next day would bring. This monument marks the spot where the pair met. (ddm)

The exhausted enemy was demoralized by the loss of Albert Sidney Johnston, who had been killed that afternoon in a peach orchard. "Whoever assumed the offensive was sure to win," Grant said.

The next morning, April 7, Grant ordered Sherman to retake his camps near Shiloh Church. Despite the condition of his division, he managed to patch together a force for the task. The advance began mid-morning and went well until it met heavy resistance near the church. After a time, the advance continued. Stumbling on masked Confederate batteries in a thick wood, Sherman had a ready answer: a pair of howitzers he had found earlier. After answering the artillery challenge, the division resumed the advance with steady progress until noting that the Rebels ran in flight before them. The Confederate army started abandoning the fight and went into full retreat. The battle of Shiloh was over.

Lt. Gen. Nathan Bedford Forrest was a Confederate cavalry commander from Memphis, Tennessee. Forrest and his wife were recently disinterred from their resting place in Memphis beneath a statue of the general. Their remains were reinterred at the National Confederate Museum in Columbia, Tennessee. (loc)

The weary Union troops did little to pursue the fleeing Rebels that night, but Sherman took up the job on the morning of April 8. However, he plunged into Confederate Colonel Nathan Bedford Forrest's ambush at Fallen Timbers. Union infantry responded to the emergency, and the Confederate cavalry continued the retreat. Forrest, though severely wounded in the fight, completed his own escape.

Exhausted, Sherman returned to his original camp and reclaimed the tent he had occupied before the battle. Beauregard and Bragg—his two old chums that now donned gray uniforms—had made use of the tent just the night before. Pausing now to consider the whirlwind he had just survived, Sherman mourned the loss of the 300 killed from his division. His total casualties had exceeded 2,0000 in two days, about one-quarter of his total strength. Union casualties overall numbered about 13,000, and the Confederates had just over 10,000 dead, wounded, or missing. All told—North and South—at the battle of Shiloh, 23,746 men fell. The bloodbath took time for both sides to comprehend.

Undoubtedly, Sherman had done very well. "During eight hours [on Sunday] the fate of the army depended upon the life of one man," one participant recalled, "if General Sherman had fallen, the army would have been captured or destroyed." General Halleck agreed and wrote to Secretary of War Edwin Stanton:

> It is the unanimous opinion here that Brig. Gen. W. T. Sherman saved the fortune of the day on the 6th instance and contributed largely to the glorious victory on the 7th. He was in the thickest of the fight on both days. . . . I respectfully request that he be made a major-general of volunteers.

Much to Sherman's chagrin, newspaper correspondents soon descended on the site and swarmed over the camps collecting and inventing stories, and eyewitness reports of the battle crowded the pages. "Probably no single battle of the war gave rise to such wild and damaging reports," Sherman observed later.

The 27th secretary of war, Edwin McMasters Stanton was an efficient—if ruthless—administrator during the Civil War. In 1869, President Grant named Stanton to the Supreme Court, but the new justice died before he could take his place on the bench. (loc)

> It was publicly asserted at the North that our army was taken completely by surprise; that the rebels caught us in our tents; bayoneted the men in their beds; that General Grant was drunk; that Buell's opportune

Maj. Gen. John Pope was a Union officer who enjoyed some success in the Western Theater during the Civil War before being transferred east to lead the Army of the Potomac. After a humiliating defeat at Second Bull Run, Pope was banished to Minnesota. (loc)

arrival save the Army of the Tennessee from utter annihilation, etc.

Shiloh had been a Union victory, and Grant had been in command, yet his reputation was sorely damaged. "If the news from Donelson had sent him soaring like a rocket in the public's estimation, the news from Shiloh dropped him sparkless like the stick," 20th Century writer Shelby Foote observed. The condemnation poured in, and eventually, Lincoln had to decide to sustain Grant or not. Finally, he purportedly declared, "I can't spare this man. He fights."

Once Halleck arrived at Pittsburg Landing, he assumed command of the armies: Buell's Army of the Ohio, General Pope's Army of the Mississippi, and the Army of the Tennessee. Grant, removed from command of the latter army, became second in command to Halleck, with no specific duties. Reorganizing the army scheme into wings—right, left, and center—the Union force readied a campaign against Corinth.

As the new campaign began, Sherman learned that Grant had been given a 30-day leave and was preparing to depart. Curious about this sudden turn of events, though he knew Grant felt unhappy playing second fiddle to Halleck, Sherman hastened to Grant's headquarters. He found the general packing and asked his quiet friend the meaning of it all. "Sherman, you know," Grant answered. "You know that I am in the way here. I have stood it as long as I can and can endure it no longer." He planned to visit St. Louis. The new major general asked if "if he had any business there." "Not a bit," Grant replied. Sherman saw that it was a matter of pride. He then appealed for Grant to stay. In his memoirs, the redhead recalled his argument.

> *Before the battle of Shiloh, I had been cast down by a mere newspaper assertion of "crazy;" but that single battle had given me new life, and now I was in high feather; and I argued with him that, if he went away, events would go right along, and he would be left out; whereas, if he remained, some happy accident might restore him to favor and his true place.*

The conversation convinced Grant to stay and bide his time. Sure enough, Sherman had prophetically read the situation. In early July 1862, Grant resumed his place at the head of the Army of the Tennessee, though it had been a hard wait.

That spring Halleck and his armies had inched toward Corinth with about 100,000 men. Exceedingly cautious, "Old Brains" prescribed every march, and the troops entrenched every night. After twenty-five miles in thirty days, the Union forces found the city abandoned. Beauregard and his Confederates had slipped away. It was a hollow victory, but a victory nonetheless.

While Grant returned to command in July, Sherman found a new post: military governor of Memphis, Tennessee. Likewise, Halleck climbed to a new sphere as the Army's new general-in-chief, replacing McClellan who had fallen from favor. Making his headquarters at Memphis's finest hotel, the Gayoso House, the new military governor set to the task of bringing order.

"This is Murder!"

They were all volunteers—and unmarried—those 150 Union men called the "Forlorn Hope." Powerful cannon had pounded the Confederates for four straight hours. Laden with planks and hastily built ladders, they struggled up the road in front of you. Their job: bridge the seven-foot-deep ditch that fronted the Confederate fort looming 200 yards ahead. As they moved down the open road, deadly fire from the fort cut the boys in blue to pieces.

Only a handful made it to the ditch alive, where they rem pinned down. The Union attack bogged down. A second was ordered. Again, the Federals were ripped apart as th advanced along the road. The numbing casualties of M convinced General Grant to lay siege to Vicksburg. Al the Forlorn Hope volunteers were casualties during th assault. The survivors were awarded the Medal of H

e troops back!
illiam T. Sherman

The Vicksburg Puzzle

CHAPTER SIX

JULY 1862–JULY 1863

While Sherman brought order to Memphis's chaos, Grant contemplated his next move in the autumn of 1862. He eagerly desired to go on the offensive but felt concerned by Halleck's ingrained cautiousness. Without a doubt, the highest Union priority in the Mississippi Valley focused on capturing Vicksburg, Mississippi.

The Confederacy had virtually stopped all Union steamboat traffic at Vicksburg with many large artillery pieces placed on the city's high bluff facing down over the Mississippi River below. Union commerce from the vital mid-west could not get to the markets in New Orleans. Then, there was the railroad; Vicksburg was the linchpin holding the Confederacy's single rail line linking east and west, connecting to the vital Trans-Mississippi West. Strategically, no place in the west ranked more important to the fortunes of the Confederacy, and therefore, it was the prime target for the Union to seize. Capturing Vicksburg would reopen the Mississippi River to commerce while at the same time cutting the Confederacy in two.

During the summer, the Union navy had tried to reduce the bluff-top citadel but failed in the attempt. Despite bringing more than 200 guns to bear against the Confederate batteries, the navy met with stalemate and dropped back down river. Writing to Secretary of War Edwin Stanton, Halleck assured him that if the navy "fail[ed] to take Vicksburg, I will send an expedition for that purpose."

Sherman's men made ill-fated assaults against Stockade Redan on May 19 and again on May 22, 1863, as part of Grant's initial attempts to take Vicksburg. (cm)

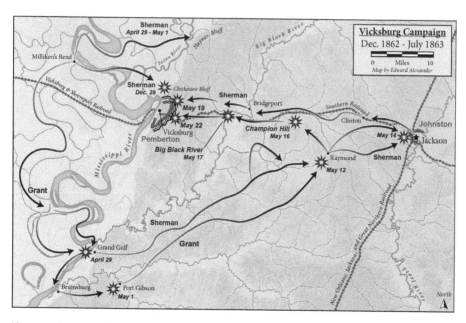

VICKSBURG CAMPAIGN—The Vicksburg Campaign was one of the longest and most difficult military campaigns for Grant and the Army of the Tennessee. For Sherman, it was a test of his patience and loyalty to Grant.

Union Maj. Gen. John A. McClernand was a Democratic Congressman from Illinois before the war and friend of President Abraham Lincoln. (loc)

During the early fall, Grant suspected intrigue in his department. Major General John A. McClernand had his eyes on Vicksburg and eagerly planned to make himself a Union war hero to further his political ambitions. An Illinois lawyer and politician, McClernand was a friend of Lincoln and attempted to leverage that connection to secure a special command, allowing him to capture the bluff-top citadel. The president and secretary of war gave the intensely ambitious general the go-ahead, and McClernand lost no time venturing back to the mid-west to recruit his Army.

Allowing McClernand to operate within Grant's department without his knowledge and consulting him was short-sighted and a bad idea from the start. Additionally, Halleck had not been consulted, and he was general-in-chief of the army. In early November, Halleck confirmed by a message the rumors Grant had heard, saying, "Memphis will be made the depot of a joint military and naval expedition on Vicksburg."

Grant was incredulous. "Am I to understand that I lie still here," the taciturn general inquired, "while an expedition is fitted out from Memphis?" He needed to understand the scope of his authority given this new development. "Am I to have Sherman move

The city of Vicksburg, Mississippi, was founded by the Methodist parson Newitt Vick in 1825. (loc)

subject to my order, or is he and his forces reserved for some special service?" Although cagey and incomprehensible at times, Halleck was also unhappy with McClernand's venture and on Grant's side this time. Asserting his authority, Halleck told Grant, "You have command of all troops sent to your department and have permission to fight the enemy where you please." Reassured, Grant began planning his own Vicksburg campaign.

On November 15, Grant summoned Sherman to a meeting in Kentucky. Already aware of McClernand's intrigues, the Memphis military governor was ready for anything. Sherman loathed politician generals right alongside meddlesome journalists. Moreover, Sherman remembered their Shiloh service together and was unimpressed. As historian Brian Holden Reid explained, Sherman believed, "McClernand was nothing but a bombastic, shallow glory-seeker of mediocre military judgement." When he arrived in Columbus, Grant briefed Sherman on his plan

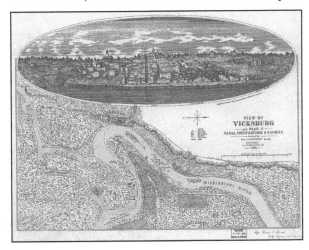

Located on bluffs overlooking the Mississippi River, Vicksburg was able to stop Union commercial traffic on the river by placing artillery on the commanding heights. (loc)

LEFT: Maj. Gen. William Tecumseh Sherman was rarely found in a proper uniform. On campaign, you were likely to find him wearing an old coat and brown corduroy pants. (loc)

RIGHT: A graduate of the U.S. Military Academy at West Point, Union Maj. Gen. James B. McPherson served in the U.S. Army Corps of Engineers before the war, aiding the construction of Fort Delaware. (loc)

of operations. Sherman should leave a garrison in Memphis and march with his remaining troops "to aim for the Tallahatchie, so as to come up on his right by a certain date." Troops from Corinth, under the command of Major General James B. McPherson, would also join the expedition.

Leaving Maj. Gen. Stephen Hurlbut in command of Memphis, Sherman "marched out of Memphis punctually with three small divisions." By early December, Grant had assembled his army of about 40,000 and readied to move against Confederate Lt. Gen. John Pemberton, who had placed his army below the Tallahatchie River. But upon arriving at the river, Grant and Sherman found that the Rebels had fallen back.

Evolving a new plan and mindful of the need for celerity if his plan to circumvent McClernand would work, Grant sent Sherman back to Memphis with new orders. He would hold Pemberton in front, while Sherman worked his way downriver and with the cooperation of the navy "proceed to the reduction of . . . [Vicksburg] in such a manner as circumstances and your own judgement may dictate." Sherman saw that he was being given the opportunity of a lifetime.

Rear Admiral David Dixon Porter, commanding the Mississippi River Squadron, proved to be an invaluable partner over the next six months. With his help, Sherman and his army arrived at Milliken's Bend, Louisiana, on Christmas Day 1862 and began preparations for the drive against the "Gibraltar of the West."

A detailed reconnaissance demonstrated unmistakably to Sherman that Grant had given him

LEFT: Maj. Gen. Stephen A. Hurlbut was born in Charleston, South Carolina, where he was raised and studied law. Later, Hurlbut moved to Illinois, where he was elected to the Illinois House of Representatives in 1859. (loc)

RIGHT: Born in Philadelphia, Pennsylvania, Lt. Gen. John C. Pemberton nevertheless joined the Confederate army during the Civil War. (loc)

an incredibly difficult assignment. The lay of the land was a nightmare for military operations. Though great for defense, a military offensive would be "as difficult as it could possibly be from nature and art," the frustrated redhead complained. The attack, launched on December 29, ended with a bloody repulse. The battle of Chickasaw Bluffs cost the Rebels less than 200 men, while Sherman's casualties numbered almost 1,800.

"Well," Sherman wrote Ellen, "we have been to Vicksburg, and it was too much for us, and we have backed out." Dejected by the failed effort, the melancholy redhead consoled himself that the topography of the area worked against him. He also assumed Pemberton had reinforced Vicksburg as he launched his assault. Rumor suggested that the Rebels had captured and destroyed the Union depot at Holly Springs and that Grant had pulled back. Now, the direction of affairs fell from Sherman's hands. "McClernand has arrived to Supersede me," the Ohio general wrote glumly, "by order of the President himself."

Miffed by what he saw as Grant's attempt to pull the carpet out from under him, McClernand hastily took command of the army at Milliken's Bend. After renaming the army the "Army of the Mississippi," the ambitious former congressman formulated a plan to capture a minor Confederate fort upriver called Arkansas Post. This effort commenced on January 11th and Sherman was proud of the success. "As usual my troops had the fighting and did the work but of course others will claim the merit and the Glory," Sherman wrote, "Let them have it. The soldiers

A Union war hero, Adm. David Dixon Porter was only the second man promoted to the rank of full admiral. Following the war, Porter served as Superintendent of the U.S. Naval Academy. (loc)

Currier and Ives print of *The Bombardment and Capture of Fort Hindman, Arkansas Post.* Fought in January 1863, the Union battle was Maj. Gen. John McClernand's only victory while he was in independent command. (loc)

know who studied the ground ahead and direct the movement."

On January 18, Grant arrived to command the expedition in person. Reorganizing the troops in the Departments of Tennessee and Missouri created four new army corps. McClernand would command the XIII Corps, Sherman the XV, while the XVI would be under Hurlbut, and McPherson would lead the XVII. All reported to Grant. Reduced essentially to just one of four subordinate commanders, McClernand chafed and complained to Washington only to be told that Grant was in charge.

Gladdened by Grant's arrival and not unhappy to see McClernand knocked down a few pegs, Sherman knew a hard winter of work lay ahead. As historian Brooks Simpson explained, Sherman "grew despondent about the war effort to the point that once more he spoke of resigning his commission, something he always mentioned when he was extremely frustrated." Any number of schemes were attempted, sometimes by the army, sometimes by the navy, but to no end. Vicksburg, it seemed, sat there taunting them. "Here we are at Vicksburg," Sherman wrote Ellen, "on the wrong side of the river trying to turn the Mississippi by a ditch, a pure waste of human labor."

As Sherman fumed, Grant planned and "having caught what he believed was a gleam of victory through the haze of cigar smoke in the former ladies' cabin of

[his headquarters boat] the *Magnolia*, was putting the final improvisatorial touches to a plan of campaign that would open, two days later, with a crossing of the greatest river of them all." Evincing an audacity that surprised his subordinates, and especially Sherman, Grant determined to cross his entire army from the west bank of the big river to the east bank and to then operate against Vicksburg from the south and west without a reliable supply line. Already the stoic commander had caused the navy squadron to run the batteries of Vicksburg—a harrowing adventure threatening disaster but navigated without significant loss—to ferry the army to the left bank. Grant had had enough scheming to find a way around Vicksburg; now, he was going at the city in deadly earnest.

Sherman did not like Grant's new plan one wit. "My own opinion is that this whole plan of attack on Vicksburg will fail must fail, and the fault will be on us all of course," he wrote Ellen. His preference, instead, was a return to Memphis and a move overland in a more orthodox fashion. "I confess I don't like this roundabout project," he fumed, "but we must support Grant in whatever he undertakes." Clearly, Sherman meant it because his loyalty was tested almost immediately. As a diversion, the snappish general had to make a convincing feint against Haynes Bluff— the stoutest part of the Confederate defenses—to draw attention away from the crossing of the army

Just after 9:00 p.m. on April 16th, a Union flotilla commanded by Acting Rear Adm. David Dixon Porter successfully passed the Vicksburg batteries, losing only one transport. This set the stage for a new army campaign to capture the hilltop citadel. (wc)

Joseph Eggleston Johnston was already a general before the Civil War began, serving as the quartermaster general of the U.S. Army. When the Confederacy created the rank of full general, Johnston found himself outranked by three other men—despite outranking them all in the old army. It turned him into a passionate critic of Confederate president Jefferson Davis, who made the appointments. (loc)

The capital of Mississippi during the Civil War, Jackson was founded in 1821 and named in honor of Andrew Jackson. Sherman's corps was charged with destruction of the city's military infrastructure on May 15, 1863. (hw)

downstream. "This diversion, made with so much pomp and display . . . completely fulfilled its purpose," Sherman wrote later, allowing the army to gain the foothold it needed on the eastern shore.

Instead of moving directly on Vicksburg, Grant determined first to swing east to avoid getting trapped against the Big Black River. He then resolved to move north to cut the railroad between Vicksburg and Jackson, thus cutting off Pemberton's main supply route. Grant unexpectedly ran into Confederates at Raymond on May 12, which then prompted a spur-of-the-moment decision to move on Jackson, the state capital, before resuming his drive on the main target. In this course, the XV Corps played a considerable role. On May 14, McPherson and Sherman assaulted Jackson, where Confederate General Joe Johnston was already in the midst of an evacuation. The rebels pulled back into entrenchments to buy time, but Sherman used the 95th Ohio Infantry to flank the position. Johnston slipped away just in time, but left eighteen guns behind.

Calling together his corps commanders at the Bowen House, Jackson's premier hotel just across from the state house, Grant anxiously wanted to press the army's momentum. "He had intercepted dispatches from Pemberton to Johnston," Sherman recalled, "which made it important for us to work smart to prevent a junction of their respective forces." Sherman "was ordered to remain one day to break up railroads, to destroy the arsenal, a foundry, the cotton-factory . . . and then to follow McPherson." Already a practiced hand at wrecking railroads, Sherman was destined to become an expert at the craft.

Sherman was finishing the business at the Mississippi capital when Grant summoned him. The XV Corps missed participating in the Union victory at the battle of Champion Hill but joined the army in time for the Battle of Big Black River on May 17.

DESTRUCTION OF REBEL PROPERTY AT JACKSON, MISSISSIPPI, MAY 16.

Crossing upstream, Sherman flanked the Confederate army, and the rebels fled, not stopping until they reached the protection of the Vicksburg defenses.

The Union army closed rapidly on Vicksburg and prepared to assault the works. Grant's first concern, however, focused on securing a supply base on the Yazoo River above Vicksburg. Sherman stared down the Walnut Hills, looking in reverse at the very position he tried to carry in December. Then Grant arrived. "He turned to me," Grant recalled in his memoirs, "saying that up to this minute he had felt no positive assurance of success." Turning effusive, the passionate redhead declared that "this . . . was the end of one of the greatest campaigns in history."

Shelby Foote, in his iconic *The Civil War: A Narrative*, summarized the Union army's remarkable success that so buoyed Sherman:

In the twenty days since they crossed the Mississippi, they had marched 180 miles to fight and win five

The battle of Champion Hill was sketched by artist Theodore Russell Davis for *Harper's Weekly*. (hw)

The siege of Vicksburg lasted from May 18th until July 4th, 1863. Instead of incarcerating the men of the Confederate army surrendered by General Pemberton, General Grant decided to parole the entire garrison. (wc)

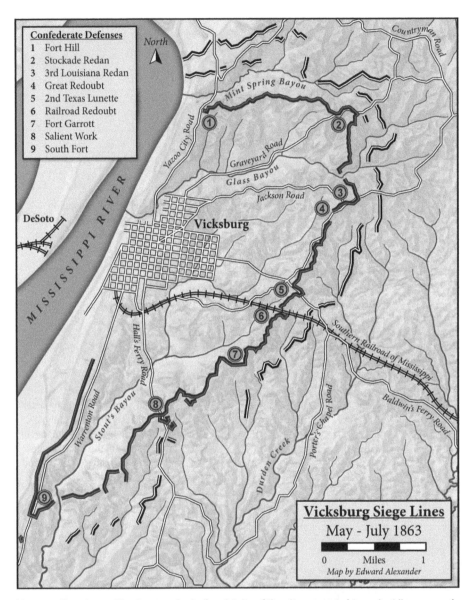

Confederate Defenses
1   Fort Hill
2   Stockade Redan
3   3rd Louisiana Redan
4   Great Redoubt
5   2nd Texas Lunette
6   Railroad Redoubt
7   Fort Garrott
8   Salient Work
9   South Fort

Vicksburg Siege Lines
May - July 1863

0   Miles   1
Map by Edward Alexander

Vicksburg Siege Lines—The topography in the vicinity of the city amounted to a giant jigsaw puzzle that the Union army had to put together piece by piece. (wc)

battles—*Port Gibson, Raymond, Jackson, Champion Hill, Big Black River—occupy a Deep South capital, inflict over 7000 casualties at a cost of less than 4500 of their own, and seize no less than fifty pieces of field artillery . . . they had not lost a gun or a stand of colors, and they had never failed to take an assigned objective.*

Coonskin Tower at Vicksburg was the brainchild of Union Lt. Henry C. Foster of the 22nd Indiana Infantry. An expert marksman with a creative impulse, Foster built the tower to get a better angle to snipe at the Rebel lines. (wc)

Grant never wanted a siege. He preferred to storm the bluff-top fortress and finish the business. The rebels were, after all, exhausted and demoralized by defeat. Sherman and all the corps commanders joined Grant's belief that they should assault. They did, twice—on May 19 & 22—and failed. As it turned out, the Confederates were not as demoralized as supposed, especially the garrison troops who had never ventured out of the city. Moreover, the Union Army had not considered the "very difficult ground, cut up by almost impracticable ravines, and line of entrenchments." The Union army settled in for a siege.

Although regretting the twin repulses, Sherman noted that Grant scored one victory—over McClernand. "Ever full of himself," biographer James Lee McDonough wrote, "[McClernand] finally went too far, even for Grant's patience." The problem stemmed from a congratulatory order the Illinois politician-general issued to his corps. It claimed an inordinate share of the glory during the campaign for Vicksburg, which soon found its way into the newspapers—as McClernand no doubt intended. Sherman was livid. The order suggested that Sherman and McPherson had disobeyed orders from Grant on May 22 during the assault on Vicksburg—which the fiery redhead characterized as a "monstrous falsehood." After verifying the facts, Grant finally disposed of McClernand, replacing him with Maj. Gen. Edward O. C. Ord.

Siege operations continued as the Union army swelled to near 75,000. They believed Pemberton had about 30,000 Confederates in the city. Beyond the Big Black River hovered Joe Johnston, gathering an army to come to Vicksburg's relief. Sherman recalled Grant saying that Johnston "was about the only general on that side whom he feared." With that in mind, in late June, Grant decided to employ a newly arrived corps under General J. G. Parke to create a rearward-facing

Union Maj. Gen. Edward Otho Cresap Ord had the reputation for being a mathematical genius. At the U.S. Military Academy at West Point, Ord was Sherman's roommate for a time. (loc)

LEFT: **Maj. Gen. Frederick Steele was a Union officer during the Civil War and served under Sherman in the XV Corps during the siege of Vicksburg. He commanded the First Division.** (loc)

RIGHT: **Confederate Secretary of War James A. Seddon was one of five men to serve in that post during the war. He was the longest-serving Confederate Secretary of War with a tenure of two years.** (na)

Union Maj. Gen. Nathaniel Prentice Banks was the former governor of Massachusetts and had been speaker of the U.S. House of Representatives prior to the war. (loc)

line to dissuade Johnston from coming to Pemberton's aid. Sherman was placed in command and given his choice of a division from the other corps to supplement Parke. General Steele temporarily took charge of the XV Corps.

The Confederate government in Richmond frantically worried that Vicksburg might be lost. They pressed Johnston repeatedly to try anything at any cost to save the citadel. Finally, on June 15, Johnston wired Confederate Secretary of War Seddon, "The odds against me are much greater than those you express. I consider saving Vicksburg hopeless." With that message, Richmond began to see more clearly: Johnston would not even try. According to Michael Ballard, author of *Vicksburg: The Campaign that Opened the Mississippi*, "Johnston, lacking interest in the matter, did nothing, and an impotent Confederate government could do nothing about it. Pemberton and his army were on their own."

On July 4, 1863—Independence Day—John Pemberton surrendered the city of Vicksburg to Grant. Several Confederate officers protested their commander's decision to surrender on that day, but Pemberton answered that he could get better terms.

A view of the Mississippi River from the City of Vicksburg. (wc)

Print from *Harper's Pictorial History of the Civil War* depicting a discussion between Union general Ulysses S. Grant and Confederate general John C. Pemberton between the lines during the siege of Vicksburg. Pemberton's capitulation soon followed. (loc)

Sherman had hoped "Grant would have given me Vicksburg and let some one else follow up the enemy inland," but that was not to be. As ordered, the wizened warrior followed his superior's wishes, bade his men "give one big huzza and sling the knapsack for new fields," and set off to intercept Johnston.

Other important Union victories surrounded the fall of Vicksburg. On July 3, the battle of Gettysburg concluded after three days of horrendous fighting with a resounding Union victory. Just a few days after Vicksburg's capitulation, Port Hudson surrendered to General Nathaniel Banks, allowing the Mississippi, as Lincoln observed, to go "unvexed to the sea." These victories, Sherman observed, "should have ended the war; but the rebel leaders were mad and seemed determined that their people should drink of the very lowest dregs of the cup of war, which they themselves had prepared."

The Union victory at Vicksburg completed the rehabilitation of Sherman's reputation. Growing in public esteem, Sherman and Grant's names would increasingly be linked. The slim Ohioan, like many, at first thought the twin victories of Gettysburg and Vicksburg might spell the end of the rebellion, but Confederate intransigence would go on indefinitely. This reality hardened Sherman, who determined to show the South that he was a man of fire, in more ways than one.

This postcard depicts the second Surrender Monument of Vicksburg, which marks the site where Grant and Pemberton famously met between the lines during the siege and worked out the terms of surrender. The original Surrender Monument was heavily vandalized for souvenirs and now is on display in the National Park Service Visitor's Center. (loc)

The Grieving General

CHAPTER SEVEN

JULY 1863–JANUARY 1864

The fall of Vicksburg let the Union army sigh in relief and lifted Sherman's spirits. He felt tired but was in "high feather," as he liked to say. "The capture of Vicksburg is to me the first gleam of daylight in this war," he wrote Ellen. "Here is Glory enough for all the Heros (sic) of the West, but I content myself with Knowing & feeling that our enemy is weakened so much, and more yet by failing to hold a point deemed by them as essential to their empire in the South West."

As directed, Sherman marched to chase Johnston out of Mississippi. It did not take a lot of convincing since Johnston had the same idea. That done, the Ohio general turned his attention to finishing the destruction of Jackson and the railroad. Exhausted and cynical, Sherman perceived that his reputation had carved a niche for him. "It is now magnificently accomplished, and here I would seek repose," he told his wife. "But no—it has been ever thus, when desperate schemes are in contemplation, or pursuit after battle Sherman is called for. He don't mind abuse, has no political aspirations, and moves with celerity—Therefore I am the man for any and every emergency."

Sherman's star was rising fast. Assistant Secretary Charles Dana exclaimed, "What a splendid soldier he is." When he learned he had been promoted to brigadier general in the regular army, he knew he had a place, come what may. He was an army commander, not a lawyer or a banker. "Order and stability had

A spectacular view of Chattanooga from Point Park atop Lookout Mountain. (ddm)

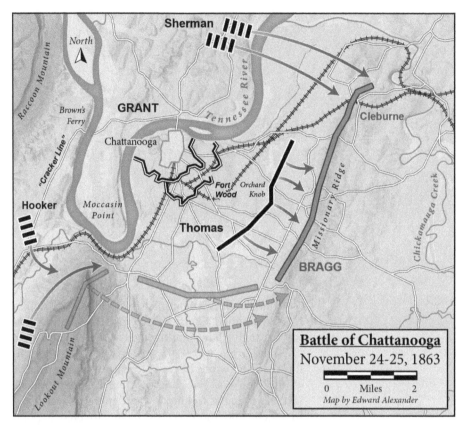

North

Raccoon Mountain

Sherman

GRANT

Brown's Ferry

"Cracker Line"

Chattanooga

Tennessee River

Cleburne

Hooker

Moccasin Point

Fort Wood

Orchard Knob

Missionary Ridge

Chickamauga Creek

Thomas

BRAGG

Lookout Mountain

Battle of Chattanooga
November 24-25, 1863

0   Miles   2
Map by Edward Alexander

BATTLE OF CHATTANOOGA—The battle for Chattanooga was one of the most challenging assignments of Sherman's career. Positioned on the north end of Missionary Ridge, the redhead could make little progress against Confederate forces. Later, both Grant and Sherman would claim that Sherman's action drew Confederate troops from the center, allowing Thomas to break Bragg's line.

finally been achieved," Marszalek wrote, "and reigned in his family as it did in the war itself."

Finally, Sherman got the repose he so desperately needed. His family joined him in August, and they all enjoyed a fine camp near the Big Black River. The conviviality and socializing lasted into the early fall. Cump's children played and gathered souvenirs from the battlefield. There was time for pondering, too, and Sherman did plenty of that. His notions of war were evolving. When Halleck reached out for his thoughts on reconstruction, the eccentric general responded mercilessly. He stood entirely against allowing civilian governments in any state that had seceded. "They had a government so mild and paternal that they gradually forgot they had any at all . . . they asserted an absolute right to seize public moneys, forts, arms, and even to shut up the natural avenues of travel and commerce.

They chose war—they ignored and denied all the obligations of the solemn contract of government and appealed to force," he later explained in his memoirs.

Sherman bitterly blamed the Southern people for the war—not just the politicians and Confederate military. Moreover, he differed from many who viewed war as only against armed men. Sherman saw war as total—all-encompassing. He wrote:

> *I would banish all minor questions, assert the broad doctrine that as a nation the United States has the right, and also the physical power, to penetrate to every part of our national domain, and that we will do it— that we will do it in our own time and in our own way; that it makes no difference whether it be in one year, or two, or ten, or twenty; that we will remove and destroy every obstacle, if need be, take every life, every acre of land, every particle of property, everything that to us seems proper; that we will not cease till the end is attained; that all who do not aid us are enemies, and that we will not account to them for our acts. If the people of the South oppose, they do so at their peril; and if they stand by, mere lookers-on in this domestic tragedy, they have not right to immunity, protection, or share in the final result . . . .*

> *I would not coax them, or even meet them half-way, but make them so sick of war that generations would pass away before they would again appeal to it.*

Union Maj. Gen. William S. Rosecrans fancied himself an amateur theologian who enjoyed late night debates with his staff. (loc)

Sherman's unofficial furlough beside the Big Black River came to a sudden, disturbing end as September 1863 drew to a close. Word arrived on September 22 that the Army of the Cumberland had been routed in north Georgia at the battle of Chickamauga, September 18-20. Limping back to the defenses of Chattanooga, Union commander William Rosecrans soon found himself and his army virtually surrounded and his supply lines cut. Confederate General Braxton Bragg, commanding the Army of Tennessee, had Rosecrans in a tight spot with infantry and artillery on all the surrounding heights, staring down at the wounded Union force.

Sherman's old friend, George Thomas, had saved the Army of the Cumberland from utter annihilation. As the left and center of the Union army collapsed, Thomas's corps took the brunt of the whole Confederate army to buy time for the

Union Maj. Gen. George
H. Thomas was a native
of Virginia and West Point
graduate who shared a room
at the academy with Sherman.
A former slave owner, Thomas
remained loyal to the Union
when war broke out. (loc)

rest to escape before skillfully withdrawing himself, largely unpursued.

Ordered to send a division immediately, Grant and Sherman huddled as they gathered intelligence about the situation at Chattanooga. Meanwhile, Cump's family prepared to head home. "The whole country seemed paralyzed by this unhappy event," Sherman recorded years later, "the authorities in Washington were thoroughly stampeded." Grant determined the emergency required that Sherman send two of his remaining three divisions to Chattanooga. He would move to Memphis and then overland eastward, repairing rail lines as his troops advanced.

The flurry of activity and concern for Rosecrans's army kept Sherman busy. On the way to Memphis, aboard the steamer *Atlantic*, the general's nine-year-old son, Willie, showed symptoms of typhoid fever, which grew worse as they neared their destination. There, at the Gayoso Hotel, Willie died on October 3. He had deteriorated rapidly, and the doctors could do little. "The blow was a terrible one to us all," the grieving father wrote, "so sudden and so unexpected, that I could not help reproaching myself for having consented to his visit in that sickly region in the summer-time." He feared he had failed Willie as a father.

As Sherman did his best to suppress his grief and attend to his duty, the Union high command seemed to move heaven and earth, trying to answer the crisis in Chattanooga. In mid-October, Grant was elevated to command of the Military Division of the Mississippi. Sherman took the lead with the Army of the Tennessee. Immediately, the War Department pressed Grant to decide to sustain Rosecrans in command at

Part of the Cumberland
Plateau, Lookout Mountain
is a mountain ridge that
straddles the Tennessee
state border with Georgia.
The mountain seems to loom
ominously above the City of
Chattanooga. (loc)

A vital Confederate railroad hub, Chattanooga, Tennessee, was always considered a strategic location during the war. (loc)

Chattanooga or replace him with George Thomas. Without hesitation, Grant chose Thomas and wired him to "hold Chattanooga at all hazards." Thomas answered, "We will hold the town till we starve."

Sherman faced a logistical nightmare as he did his best to move his army toward Chattanooga. The progress was slow but steady. With guerrillas prowling, Confederate cavalry roaming, and railroad tracks needing tending, the supply routes had been drawn and redrawn. Nothing happened easily in this effort. Then Grant summoned Sherman to Chattanooga, which the fatigued redhead reached on November 15. Soon after, the disheveled general got his first look at the situation. Standing on the parapet of Fort Wood, it seemed like standing at the bottom of a great bowl and staring up at the sides—Lookout Mountain loomed over the town, and Missionary Ridge stretched miles upriver. The view was astonishing. "Why, General Grant," Sherman exclaimed, "you are besieged." Puffing on a cigar, Grant answered, "It is too true."

After arriving in Chattanooga, Grant made his headquarters at the corner of 1st and Walnut Streets in a home owned by T. J. Lattner. (wc)

Left: Confederate Lt. Gen. James Longstreet had hoped, when he was transferred West from Lee's Army of Northern Virginia to the Army of Tennessee, to replace Braxton Bragg in command and intrigued without success with Bragg's subordinates to bring this about. (loc)

RIGHT: Union Maj. Gen. Joseph Hooker was the former commander of the Army of the Potomac. Hooker had a high opinion of himself, which led to a reputation for resigning in huff when he did not get his way. (loc)

While the supply problem was dire, Grant had already set into motion a plan to remedy the situation. With the assistance and ingenuity of General W. F. Smith, acting in the capacity of staff engineer, the "cracker line," as soldiers called it, soon started operations. That solved, Grant anxiously looked for opportunities to go on the offensive. Here, speed was essential because Bragg had dispatched Gen. James Longstreet, who had come west from the Army of Northern Virginia to Knoxville to bag Burnside's army. Grant believed a strike at Bragg would result in Longstreet's recall.

Sherman's army began to arrive at Chattanooga via the Cracker Line. Also, General Joseph Hooker approached with more Union troops; Hooker had been sent west, thanks to the energetic, highly efficient, and forceful Secretary of War Edwin Stanton. Grant had about 75,000 men—almost twice the strength of the Confederate force under Bragg (with Longstreet detached). The plan, as delineated by James Lee McDonough, placed Hooker on the right, Thomas in the center facing Missionary Ridge, and Sherman on the left. Sherman would cross the "Tennessee River several miles upstream from Chattanooga, and assault

During the battle of Chattanooga, the headquarters of the Army of the Cumberland, commanded by George Thomas, was in the Richardson House—a Greek Revival mansion on Walnut Street in Chattanooga. (wc)

Sherman's headquarters in Chattanooga. Shortly before arriving in Chattanooga, Sherman was promoted to command of the Army of the Tennessee. (wc)

the northern end of Missionary Ridge, breaking the enemy's right flank, and then advancing south along the ridge to cut the Rebel line of retreat."

If the Union commanders had known the condition and affairs on the Confederate side, they might not have been so gloomy. Bragg's army—or the senior commanders—walked dangerously near mutiny. In fact, Longstreet had been sent away partially because of his role in the machinations against Bragg. In any case, the rebel army's organization and strength faced disarray because of the losses suffered at Chickamauga—nearly 20,000. The long gray line stood thin, practically inviting Grant to break it.

Sherman's share in the battles for Chattanooga featured one problem after another. The crossing of the river on November 24 happened after many delays, then the terrain baffled him, and his troops plunged

Scene of Sherman's attack on the north end of Missionary Ridge at Tunnel Hill above Chattanooga. (wc)

Drawn by artist Alfred R. Waud, this scene depicts the battle of Missionary Ridge on the north end of the line. (loc)

Confederate Maj. Gen. Patrick R. Cleburne was an Irish-born former officer of the 41st Regiment of Foot in the British Army. In 1864, Cleburne authored a proposal for slave emancipation, which earned him the enmity of many in the Confederate army. (loc)

Like Joe Hooker, Union Maj. Gen. Ambrose Burnside was another failed former commander of the Army of the Potomac who was sent West. After the war, Burnside was elected governor of Rhode Island and then elected to the U.S. Senate. (loc)

toward a spur of Missionary Ridge—not the true objective. After reaching the correct position, they had the misfortune to run into the division commanded by General Patrick Cleburne—a tenacious Irish-born fighter widely admired as one of the best in the Confederacy. Battle on this front swayed back and forth, essentially a stalemate.

On the other end of the line, Hooker's men had better luck, capturing Lookout Mountain only to stall on the south end of Missionary Ridge. Then, Grant sent Thomas's army against the center. The original idea would put pressure on the center, but success followed success as the troops just kept going past successive lines of entrenchments. Confederate troops panicked and fled, and Thomas's army charged up and over the ridge, breaking the gray line. Bragg's men fled headlong into the valley beyond. The Union's Army of the Cumberland, seemingly demoralized by their Chickamauga thrashing, rose to the occasion, and won the day.

After dark on the battle day, Sherman learned many details of the victory. With Chattanooga secured, Grant turned his planning to assisting Burnside at Knoxville. Though besieged by Longstreet's army, the Union commander thought he could hold out for 10 to 12 days before his rations gave out. Grant originally planned to send Gordon Granger with about 20,000 men toward Knoxville, but on November 29, Sherman received a dispatch with new orders. "Granger is on the way to Burnside's relief, but I have lost all faith in his energy or capacity to manage an expedition of the importance of this one," Grant explained. "I am inclined to think, therefore, I shall have to send you." Once again, as Sherman had observed before, he was the "man for any and every emergency."

Reluctantly, Sherman set in motion plans to relieve Burnside. "That any man should send a force into East Tennessee puzzles me," the exhausted redhead wrote Grant. "Burnside is there and must be relieved, but when relieved I want to get out, and he should come out too." The last thing he wanted was to be stuck there.

Sherman took a substantial force for the mission—two divisions from the XV Corps, Howard's XI Corps, and the IV Corps under Granger. They would have to cover 120 miles in three days in bitterly cold weather. It would be a difficult march, but failure was not an option. Determined to be rescuers, most of Sherman's force arrived at Maryville, just 15 miles from Knoxville, by December 4. There, according to Brian Holden Reid, "a message arrived from Burnside announcing that Longstreet had given up his siege and withdrawn toward Virginia."

Arriving on December 6, Sherman found Burnside and his staff comfortably lodged in a fine old mansion. "We all sat down to a good dinner, embracing roast-turkey. There was a regular dining-table, with clean table-cloth, dishes, knives, forks, spoons," the incredulous general remembered later. "I had seen nothing of this kind in my field experience and could not help exclaiming that I thought they were starving." Irked by the notion that he drove his exhausted men for nothing, Sherman still felt relieved that the emergency was over and he could return to Chattanooga. Soon, his whole army would be lodged in winter quarters while Sherman began planning for the spring 1864 campaign.

The view of Missionary Ridge from Orchard Knob, where Grant and Thomas made their headquarters during the battle of Chattanooga. From this vantage point, Grant watched the Army of the Cumberland attack the center of the Confederate line. (wc)

As 1863 closed, Sherman had much from the military scenes to remember proudly. While the Vicksburg campaign had been long and frustrating at times, it was a great victory—both for the Union and for himself. Chattanooga and Knoxville had been relieved, though his performance in the first place had been subpar. Clearly, Grant had come to trust and depend upon his fellow Ohioan. And Sherman had substantially grown in the public's estimation. His promotion to command of the Army of the Tennessee marked an important acknowledgment of his worth as a general.

Yet 1863 had also taxed the wiry general's physical, emotional, and mental systems. By January 1864, Sherman sorely needed rest and time to heal. The loss of Willie was shocking—life-altering—but he had been given no time to grieve. A dark cloud still hung over him. Even while the eccentric commander gained new confidence professionally, finally feeling like he deserved the stars on his shoulders, privately, he battled doubts about his fitness as a parent, blaming himself for the loss of his son. Sherman returned to Lancaster in Ohio to spend Christmas with his family. It was a bittersweet yuletide reunion while the rising hero rested and readied for what was to come.

Union Maj. Gen. Gordon Granger first came to prominence at the battle of Chickamauga, but more recently is known for his General Order No. 3 in Galveston, Texas, in June 1865 when he informed the citizens of the Emancipation Proclamation. This act inspired the federal holiday marking the occasion, known as Juneteenth. (loc)

A Return to Georgia

CHAPTER EIGHT

JANUARY 1864–SEPTEMBER 1864

Returning to duty in January 1864 aboard the gunboat *Juliet*, Sherman noted much ice in the river as he steamed down to Memphis after his Christmas furlough. Guerrillas along the river, and Confederate cavalry causing mayhem, took first place in his mind for part of the journey. "It is exceedingly difficult," the shivering commander wrote his wife, "to deal with these Mounted Devils and I am sure all we can do is to make the country feel that the people must pay for these wandering Arabs." He was also considering a raid on Meridian, Mississippi, and Selma, Alabama— important Southern rail and industrial hubs.

Sherman's raid on Meridian has often been seen as a warm-up for what would come later. Historians have seen in this expedition a kind of experimentation as the fiery general tested the viability of his changing notions of warfare. Indeed, the raid had little to do with fighting Confederate armies—though he did expect resistance. Instead, the goals were to damage the resources used to sustain the rebel war effort and to influence Confederate morale.

Sherman took two army corps—the XVI and the XVII—on the raid. With a strength of over 25,000 men, the force set out from Vicksburg in late January on their 150-mile sojourn. Sherman demanded the columns travel light; no tents or extra baggage was allowed. Moreover, once they crossed the Big Black River, he planned to abandon their supply lines and live off the country. Supplementing this force rode

"The Dead Angle" along the Kennesaw Line sat atop a high ridge. Federals approached the Confederate position across open ground, uphill, in miserable heat. (cm)

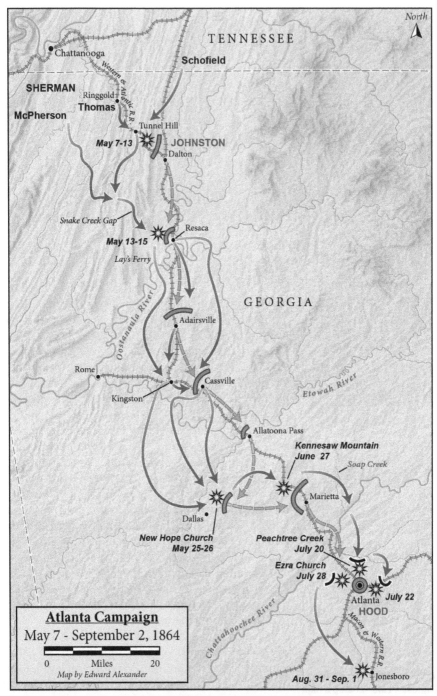

ATLANTA CAMPAIGN—The Atlanta Campaign originated as a campaign to bag Joe Johnston's army. The capture of Atlanta was not part of the scheme, though the destruction of its military capacity was. Later, when Atlanta was captured, it allowed Hood to turn the tables on Sherman and make him defend the Union supply line.

LEFT: **Union Brigadier General William Sooy Smith was a respected civil engineer who graduated from both Ohio University and the U.S. Military Academy at West Point.** (loc)

RIGHT: **Confederate Lt. Gen. Leonidas Polk was a second cousin of President James K. Polk. Prior to the war, Polk was a substantial slave holder in Tennessee and the Episcopal Bishop of Louisiana.** (loc)

7,000 cavalry under General W. Sooy Smith, who would try to run down Confederate General Nathan Bedford Forrest and his batch of "devils" before joining the Union army in Meridian to assist with the destruction.

After a mostly uneventful march for the infantry columns, they arrived in Meridian on February 14, "almost without firing a shot." The Confederate department commander, General Leonidas Polk, discounted rumors of the Union raid before vainly scattering his forces, having been fooled by Sherman's feint at Mobile. In Meridian, millions of dollars of Confederate supplies succumbed to the flames. "The supplies, the arsenal, two large hotels and gristmills were burned and the railroads for twenty-five miles in all directions were destroyed." It was a complete Union success—except that Smith's cavalry went missing.

Chastised by Forrest at Okolona, Mississippi, Smith and his cavalry slinked back to Memphis, humiliated to be bested by a force half their size. When he arrived back in Memphis and learned of the defeat, Sherman took note of Smith's cowardice for future reference, and his respect for the fighting qualities of cavalry slipped another notch.

While Sherman attended to details of his command after the Meridian campaign, he received orders to lend 10,000 troops to General Nathaniel Banks, in command at New Orleans, for an expedition up Red River, March 10 to May 22, 1864. This did not sit well with the voluble redhead, who had already started contemplating his next move. But he supposed loaning troops for 30 days would be alright, with a clear understanding that those troops be returned

Capt. Adam Badeau was a Union officer who served on General Grant's staff. After the war, Badeau wrote a magisterial three-volume biography of Grant. (loc)

Confederate Gen. Joseph E. Johnston was the grandson of Peter Johnston, an immigrant from Scotland. (loc)

on schedule. Sherman boarded a steamer for New Orleans to work out the details with Banks. He wanted to ensure there would be no misunderstanding.

Returning to Memphis, Sherman's boat was hailed, and Capt. Adam Badeau of Grant's staff boarded and presented the Ohioan with a private note from Grant. Dated March 4, the letter announced that Congress had passed a law reviving the rank of lieutenant general. Grant had been summoned to Washington in person to accept the commission. Only two other men had enjoyed this lofty rank: George Washington and, by brevet, Winfield Scott.

Grant wished to "express my thanks to you and McPherson, as the men to whom, above all others, I feel indebted for whatever I have had of success. How far your advice and suggestions have been of assistance, you know." Reaching Memphis, Sherman replied that "you do yourself injustice and us too much honor in assigning to us so large a share of the merits which have led to your high advancement." He stressed that character had been the key to his chief's success. "I believe you are as brave, patriotic, and just as the great proto-type Washington; as unselfish, kind-hearted, and honest, as a man should be; but the chief characteristic in your nature is the simple faith in success you have always manifested, which I can liken to nothing else than the faith a Christian has in his Savior."

Grant hurried east to receive his third star. As he undoubtedly anticipated, Sherman learned that he would succeed his friend as commander of the Military Division of the Mississippi. The formal transfer of command occurred when Grant returned to Nashville to tie up loose ends. Much to his dismay, the nervous redhead learned that Grant intended to return east. "Do not stay in Washington," Sherman had written his reticent friend. "Halleck is better qualified than you are to stand the buffets of intrigue and policy. Come out West." The newly minted lieutenant general explained that he had no intention of staying in Washington. He planned to make his headquarters in the field, directing the Army of the Potomac's operations in person. Though mollified, Sherman was still concerned about his friend.

At Nashville and Cincinnati, the two generals conferred about the spring campaign. Sherman's orders were "to move against Johnston's army, to break it up and get into the interior of the enemy's country as far as you can, inflicting all the damage you can against their War resources." Grant and the Army of the Potomac would take on Robert E. Lee and the Confederate Army of Northern Virginia. Both campaigns were to move at the same time.

Sherman intended to launch the Atlanta Campaign with all three field armies: the Army of the Ohio under John Schofield, the Army of the Cumberland under George Thomas, and the Army of the Tennessee commanded by James McPherson. He ordered these forces to assemble at Chattanooga by May 5, 1864. Though a substantial force of about 100,000, it did have one weakness—a deficiency in good cavalry.

As the armies lurched into motion, Sherman had a good idea of his modus operandi, as described by Lloyd Lewis in his biography *Sherman: Fighting Prophet*: "Slow, unconquerable Thomas in the center as a bulwark against counter-attack; McPherson and Schofield, younger, more aggressive men, on the flanks with smaller, fleeter armies marching in swiftly traveled arcs, feinting, swerving, feinting again, then suddenly striking like hammers into Johnston's ribs." The campaign would be a series of maneuvers through the rugged North Georgia landscape.

The campaign did not open auspiciously. Sherman sent McPherson through Snake Creek Gap to get into Johnston's rear at Resaca. The maneuver could have allowed the Union forces the opportunity to crush Johnston's army at the outset—or at worst force him to retreat, abandoning his impregnable position. But upon reaching Resaca on May 9, McPherson hesitated when finding greater opposition than he anticipated, and he pulled back. "Such an opportunity does not occur twice in a single life," Sherman recalled in his memoirs, "but at the crucial moment McPherson seems to have been a little cautious."

When Sherman detected Johnston's abandonment of his line at Dalton, he grew concerned that more weight might fall on McPherson. He sent his whole army through Snake Creek Gap for a concentration at Resaca. Enveloping the town on the north and west, the Union army found itself facing stout entrenchments. As the battle ensued on May 15th, Sherman "caused two pontoon bridges to be laid across the Oostanaula

Union Maj. Gen. John M. Schofield was a native of Chautauqua County in New York. His father, Rev. James Schofield, was a Baptist minister and missionary. (loc)

This Georgia state historical marker recalls Union General James McPherson's lodgment in Snake Creek Gap during the Atlanta Campaign. (ddm)

Print from a lithography by Kurz & Allison (1889) depicting the battle of Resaca. (loc)

River at Lay's Ferry, about three miles below the town," threatening Johnston's line of retreat. Unable to fend off this threat to his rear, Johnston retreated under the dead of night, abandoning Resaca.

In order to keep his army supplied, Sherman's advance had to conform generally with the path of the Western and Atlantic Railroad. This single line would always be vulnerable, running back to the Union supply depots in Chattanooga and Nashville. But a mastermind of supply and logistics, Sherman had created an elaborate system, including well-trained rail repair gangs to ensure continued operation.

The Confederate army retreated south, looking for good defensive ground and perhaps a position to launch an offensive. At Allatoona Pass, Johnston thought he had found just the ground he needed. Sherman refused to cooperate in this design, however. Abandoning the railroad, the Union army crossed the Etowah River and aimed a blow at Dallas. This newest flanking attempt soon turned muddy and bloody. Short of Dallas, the rebels caught the advancing Union forces at New Hope Church on May 25–26. Before regaining the railroad, Sherman lost 1,600 casualties.

Abandoning the railroad for a time to effect a wide flanking movement worked in the end, and Johnston pulled back from the defenses of Allatoona Pass, but the cost had been high and the frustrations

Battlefield of New Hope Church in Georgia where Union general Joe Hooker's XX Corps was repulsed by one division under Confederate general John Bell Hood. (loc)

many. Now back astride the railroad, Sherman again readied his army to follow Johnston. Although he thought his Confederate opposite would pull behind the Chattahoochee River, Johnson dug in at Kennesaw Mountain instead.

In the oppressive heat at the end of June, Sherman had been stymied. The Confederate position loomed as perhaps the most difficult yet. There were no good options. Sherman's usual maneuvering posed significant risk, but so did a direct assault. "[I] am now inclined to feign on both flanks and assault the center," Sherman wrote. "It may cost us dear but in results would surpass an attempt to pass around." The agitated general also grew concerned about the army's ability to assault fortified lines. Maybe some tough love and success would give them the confidence needed for future endeavors.

The battle of Kennesaw Mountain erupted on June 27 and lasted less than three hours. The Confederates repulsed the Union forces at all points. However, on Schofield's front, where he crossed

Photo of Allatoona Pass, a deep railroad cut in the Allatoona Mountain Range in Georgia. Built in the 1840s, the cut was developed to host the Western and Atlantic Railroad. (loc)

Olley's Creek, there was a potential opportunity to threaten the rebel army's line of retreat. Sherman recognized the promise of the move and formulated a new plan. "I at once thought of moving the whole army to the railroad at a point (Fulton) about ten miles below Marietta, or to the Chattahoochee River itself." No sooner did Sherman set the plan in operation when Johnston pulled out and headed for a crossing of the Chattahoochee, with the Union army close on his heels.

"I am now 105 miles from Chattanooga," Sherman wrote his wife on June 26, "all our provisions have to come over that single road—which is almost daily broken somewhere—but thus far our supplies have been ample. We have devoured the land and our animals eat up the wheat & corn fields close—All the People retire before us, and desolation is behind. To realize what war is one should follow our tracks." In a reflective mood as he contemplated crossing the last major natural obstacle guarding Atlanta, he continued, "I begin to regard the death & mangling of a couple thousand men as a small affair, a kind of morning dash—and it may be well that we become so hardened."

LEFT: **The battle of Kennesaw Mountain was a rare example of Union General William Tecumseh Sherman's use of the frontal assault in war. The resulting Union defeat cost the federal army about three thousand casualties.** (loc)

RIGHT: **A modern view of the Confederate trenches at Kennesaw Mountain, Georgia.** (wc)

Gen. Joe Johnston's field fortifications on the Chattahoochee River were an engineering marvel. In fact, new features were created here for the first time. (pd)

Arriving on the north side of the Chattahoochee River, the Union army came upon "one of the strongest pieces of field fortification I have saw," Sherman lamented. With the help of over 1,000 slaves, the Confederates had made their position impregnable. Breath-taking in its scope, Johnston had planned for the contingency that he would need protection should he need to cross his army here. Snug in its entrenchments, the Confederate army waited and watched.

Sherman wasted no time inspecting the fortifications and began to immediately search for a crossing. He had "made up my mind to feign on the right, but actually to cross over by the left." Johnston, he knew, would be watching McPherson's movements especially carefully since, by now, a clear pattern had emerged of using his troops for such an operation. However, Schofield found the necessary crossing near where Soap Creek met the Chattahoochee. Effecting the crossing on July 8 and securing a strong foothold, Sherman waited for Johnston to pull out of his formidable entrenchments and cross the river. He did not have to wait long.

Johnston withdrew his army behind Peachtree Creek, just four tantalizing miles from downtown Atlanta. Losing all patience with Johnston's caution, Jefferson Davis sacked the dapper Virginian. He put John Bell Hood in his place, despite Robert E. Lee's warning that Hood was "all lion, none of the fox." Sherman nodded approval at the change, believing that the decision would hasten the fall of the city. Hood was, in the words of historian Robert L. O'Connell,

Battlefield of Peachtree Creek. Fought July 20, 1864, the conflict was Gen. John Bell Hood's first foray in command of the Army of Tennessee. (loc)

A view of the Confederate works in front of Atlanta. Fought July 22, 1864, the battle of Atlanta was the bloodiest of the whole campaign. (loc)

"a military caricature, calling to mind Monty Python's Black Knight, missing all his limbs and spurting blood but still fulminating aggression."

Hood knew that Davis expected him to mount a desperate defense of Atlanta, and the new commander prepared to do just that. "He'll hit you like Hell . . . before you know it," Schofield warned Sherman. Sure enough, on July 20, Hood launched a bold attack against the Army of the Cumberland along Peachtree Creek. Not well coordinated, the attack had not even had the benefit of substantial reconnaissance. As a result, Hood hit the strongest part of the Union line. Repulsed, Hood's army pulled back into the Atlanta defenses.

Far from chastened by the Peachtree Creek defeat, Hood ventured out again on July 22, sensing an opportunity. Sherman had McPherson's troops on railroad wrecking duty at Decatur when Hood saw his

Erected to the memory of Gen. James B. McPherson, this monument was placed by the U.S. Army Corps of Engineers in 1956 to mark the spot where the general was killed on July 22, 1864. (ddm)

chance. Indeed, for a time, McPherson's flank hung "in the air" and was open to a turning movement. With four divisions, Hood struck a heavy blow. As the battle threatened, McPherson was actually with Sherman at his headquarters. Suddenly, as Lloyd Lewis described it, they heard a roar of guns from an unexpected quarter, and "The two generals leaped to their feet." Sensing that his boys were under attack, McPherson jumped in the saddle and rode toward the trouble. Tragically, he galloped straight into a small party of rebels who shot him off his horse. McPherson was probably dead before he hit the ground.

Kurz and Allison lithograph of the battle of Atlanta. (loc)

Back at his headquarters, Sherman soon heard a rumor that McPherson had gone missing and was likely dead or wounded. A short time later, as the battle thundered, an ambulance arrived with the body of the Army of the Tennessee commander. Tears poured down the redhead's face and into his beard, as nearby, others ripped a door off its hinges to form a make-shift catafalque. A surgeon's brief examination revealed a ball near the heart. McPherson was just thirty-five and had been engaged to be married. Writing to Adjutant General Lorenzo Thomas later, Sherman wrote, "History tells us of but few who so blended grace and gentleness of the friend, with the dignity courage, faith and manliness of the soldier."

The battle of Atlanta fell almost exclusively on the Army of the Tennessee. After McPherson

Photograph of the City of Atlanta. By the outbreak of the Civil War, Atlanta was the fourth largest city in the South with a population of nearly 10,000. (loc)

A lawyer by trade, Union Maj. Gen. John A. Logan was an Illinois legislator who became one of the war's most successful "citizen generals." (loc)

fell, Sherman purposely allowed that army to meet the enemy without assistance from the others to avenge their fallen hero, despite the opportunity to deal a mortal blow to Hood's army with his whole force. While the battle raged ferociously, it was also fought with disorganization. Hood had been wrong about McPherson's flank being completely in the air, so his troops met conditions very different than they expected.

Sherman followed events closely—too closely sometimes. In the afternoon, when a Confederate attack threatened the cohesion of the XV Corps, Sherman called for a concentration of artillery fire, which he then oversaw. He "led the batteries in person to some high, open ground in front of our line near the Howard House, placed them in position and directed their fire," Schofield remembered, "with the aid of that terrible raking fire . . . Union troops very quickly regained the entrenchments they had lost."

Though the battle of Atlanta was a blood bath, the Union cause won a significant victory —though that victory came at a high price: Union casualties exceeded 3,700. Hood's losses are hard to compute but could hardly have been less than 10,000. Of course, McPherson's loss was irreparable. "I yield to none of earth except yourself the right to excel me in lamentations for our dead hero," Sherman wrote to McPherson's fiancée.

Once again, Sherman had little time for grieving. In fact, given the fact that his armies were poised at the gates of Atlanta, the sad commander had to quickly pick a successor to his fallen friend. General "Black Jack" Logan had taken command of the Army of the Tennessee in battle out of necessity, but Sherman wanted no more politician-generals. He preferred his army commanders to be West Pointers. With Thomas's approbation, Sherman tendered the command to Gen. O. O. Howard, whom Sherman admired for his efficiency. As it turned out, this irked Joe Hooker who expected the command. The former commander of the Army of the Potomac promptly resigned in protest. Later, Sherman recalled in his memoirs, "I did feel a sense of relief when he left us."

Sherman then formulated a plan for a "wide, circular, northern sweep around Atlanta, from the east to the west side of the city" to cut off Confederate communications and ultimately the last rail route open to the rebels—the Macon & Western Railroad. Hood tried to arrest the progress of Sherman's movement, which resulted in the battle of Ezra Church on July 28. The Army of the Tennessee beat back several attempts to break their line before the Confederate army pulled back.

Union Maj. Gen. Oliver Otis Howard was a strong advocate for the education of African Americans and after the war became the first president of Howard University in Washington, D.C. (loc)

In late August, Sherman severed the last remaining rail line into Atlanta with a bold stroke. Leaving the XX Corps to guard the railroad bridge spanning the Chattahoochee (his main supply line), Sherman set off with the remainder of his infantry for a strike at Jonesboro, 20 miles south of Atlanta. Hood, entirely confused by the movements of the Union armies, gave a delayed order to General Hardee to take two corps to Jonesboro to save the rail line. "Black Jack's" XV Corps repulsed the rebel troops, sending them back with heavy losses. Atlanta was now doomed.

On the last day of August 1864, Hood began his withdrawal. He destroyed mountains of supplies, ammunition, and rolling stock on his way out. The remainder of his army limped out of the city. On September 2, Union troops marched into Georgia's capital city. Sherman sent Halleck in Washington a simple message:

"Atlanta is ours and fairly won."

This image is one of the most iconic photos of General Sherman. Taken by photographer George N. Barnard, official photographer of the Chief Engineer's Office, Sherman sits astride his horse at Federal Fort #7 in Atlanta. (loc)

Striking for Saltwater

CHAPTER NINE
September 1864–December 1864

The capture of Atlanta was a great tonic for the morale of the North. A major railroad hub and manufacturing center, the city furnished much to the Confederate cause and accoutrements to its army. Soon after the city's fall, Sherman ensured "the glad tidings flew on the wings of electricity to all parts of the North, where the people had patiently awaited news of their husbands, sons, and brothers, away down in 'Dixie Land.'" An avalanche of accolades soon poured in.

Lincoln, who benefited most from a victory that helped secure his reelection, praised the achievement. "Major-General William T. Sherman and the gallant officers and soldiers of his command before Atlanta, for the distinguished ability and perseverance displayed in the campaign in Georgia . . . has resulted in the capture of the City of Atlanta. The marches, battles, sieges, and other military operations, that have signalized the campaign must render it famous in the annals of war and have entitled those who have participated therein to the applause and thanks of the nation."

In Virginia, Grant and the Army of the Potomac had fought Lee to a draw throughout the Overland Campaign and were in a stalemate outside Petersburg. Bolstered by Sherman's success, the General-in-Chief wrote, "In honor of your great victory, I have ordered a salute to be fired with *shotted* guns from every battery bearing upon the enemy."

A view of the Ogeechee River from Fort McAllister. An earthen-work fort built by Confederate forces and captured by Union forces under Gen. William Tecumseh Sherman in 1864, Fort McAllister is now a Georgia State Park. (ddm)

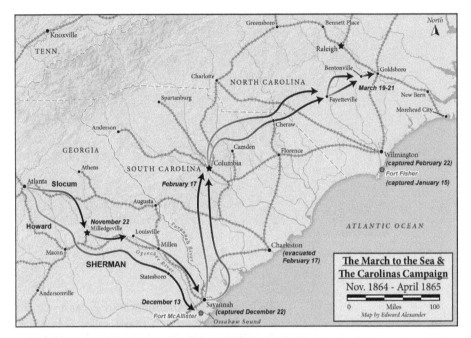

The March to the Sea & The Carolinas campaign—The March to the Sea cemented Sherman's reputation as a Union hero. In a psychological campaign against the Confederate will to continue the war and their morale, Sherman introduced a new mode of warfare.

Justly proud of his achievement, Sherman wrote to his father-in-law Thomas Ewing, "You have often said that Napoleon had no subordinate to whom he was willing to entrust an hundred thousand men & yet have lived to see the little redheaded urchin not only handle an hundred thousand men, smoothly & easily, but fight them in masses of tens and fifty thousands at a distance of hundreds of miles from his arsenals and sources of supply." This was more than boasting—it was clarifying. Sherman realized his potential, and his identity now involved command of large armies intertwined with accomplishments that would be immortalized in history. He was now a national hero. It must have been gratifying to reflect on the days when he was labeled insane and see the same papers and people hail him as a military genius.

Sherman set to work at once, destroying Atlanta's infrastructure. He believed this would require expelling the civilian population, but he knew this would be controversial. "If the people raise a howl against my barbarity and cruelty," the newly minted hero wrote Halleck, "I will answer that war is war, and not popularity seeking. If they want peace, they and their relatives must stop the war." He had seen enough of war and had grown callous and even more cynical. "I knew that the people of the South would read in this measure two important conclusions," Sherman reflected in his memoirs, "one, that we were in earnest; and the other, if they were sincere in their common and popular clamor "to die in the last ditch," that the opportunity would soon come."

Hood took exception to the expulsion of Atlanta's citizens, though he admitted, "I do not consider that I have any alternative in this matter." In a note to Sherman, arranging for a truce to effect the evacuation, the sullen Texan wrote, "Sir, permit me to say that the unprecedented measure you propose transcends, in studied and ingenious cruelty, all acts ever before brought to my attention in the dark history of war. . . . In the name of God and humanity, I protest."

Maj. Gen. William Tecumseh Sherman. Sherman was a fan of Shakespeare and often quoted from his works in conversation. (wc)

Sherman, clearly riled by Hood's missive, responded without delay.

In the name of common sense, I ask you not to appeal to a just God in such a sacrilegious manner. You who, in the midst of peace and prosperity, have plunged a nation into war—dark and cruel war—who dared and badgered us into battle, insulted our flag, seized our arsenals and forts. . . . Talk thus to the marines, but not to me who have seen these things, and who will this day make as much sacrifice for the peace and honor of the South as the best-born Southerner among you! If we must be enemies, let us be men, and fight it out as we propose to do, and not deal in such hypocritical appeals to God and humanity.

Hood was not chastened by Sherman's reply but continued the correspondence to the satisfaction of neither. Later, the Confederate general had the entire correspondence published in the newspapers—a move he knew would incense the redheaded conqueror of Atlanta. Meanwhile, the mayor of Atlanta, James M. Calhoun, also penned a letter protesting the city's evacuation. Sherman dealt with him as he had Hood, with a defense of his measures and a stinging indictment of the Confederacy. "You cannot qualify war in harsher terms than I will," the indignant general wrote.

War is cruelty, and you cannot refine it; and those who brought war into our country deserve all the curses and

*maledictions a people can pour out. . . . You might as
well appeal against the thunder-storm as against these
terrible hardships of war. They are inevitable, and the
only way the people of Atlanta can hope once more
to live in peace and quiet at home, is to stop the war,
which can only be done by admitting that it began in
error and is perpetuated in pride.*

By making his objective Atlanta and not Hood's
army, Sherman had to accept that the tables would
more or less be turned. Now, he had the burden of
defending Atlanta—and his tenuous supply line—
and Hood had the room to maneuver his army to
the best advantage. That meant attacking the Union
lines of supply and communication, something he did
with verve. For a time, the Union commander chased
Hood and his minions all over North Georgia in an
attempt to lure him out into the open—to no avail.
The frustrating exercise convinced Sherman that the
game was not worth it. Once Hood skedaddled with
his army into Alabama, the exasperated general let
him go and returned to Atlanta.

Formulating a new plan, Sherman "had come to
understand that defeat was ultimately a state of mind
and that he was in a position to utterly demoralize the
Confederacy by making it look helpless." His notion
was to leave Hood to George Thomas and the Army of
the Cumberland, then return to Nashville, and strike
out across Georgia, moving eastward and blazing a
trail of destruction all the way to the sea. In a wire to
Grant, Sherman outlined his plan and motives. "I can
make this march, and make Georgia howl! This may
not be war but statesmanship," the insightful general
contended. "If the North can march an army right
through the South, it is proof positive that the North

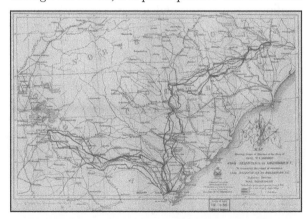

This map was prepared by the
Union War Department after
the war, showing the routes
of march for Sherman's army
during the Savannah and
Carolinas campaigns. (loc)

can prevail in this contest . . . the result operating upon the minds of sensible men would produce fruits more than compensating for the expense, trouble, and risk." The thought of leaving Hood to Thomas unsettled Grant, who saw in Thomas's track record a tendency to move ponderously. "I regard the pursuit of Hood as useless," Sherman wrote his chief. "If I turn back, the whole effect of my campaign will be lost. . . . I am clearly of the opinion that the best results will follow my contemplated movement through Georgia." Finally, on November 2, 1864, Grant conceded, "I do not see that you can withdraw from where you are to follow Hood, without giving up all we have gained in territory. I say, then, go on as you propose."

Sherman considered himself unleashed. Already, he had all the elements in place for the proposed march, so that he could execute the plan without delay. He would take just over 60,000 of the best troops culled from the Army of the Tennessee and two other corps. These he grouped into left and right wings under Henry Slocum and O. O. Howard, respectively. The army would travel light with a minimum number of wagons, cutting supply and communication lines once they left Atlanta. They would live off the country and move rapidly, tearing up railroads as they went.

The key to the success of the campaign would be deception. Feinting at Macon and Augusta, Sherman wanted to keep Confederate authorities guessing at his objectives. He planned a psychological chess match, an unorthodox game of war in which Sherman made the rules. It all got underway on November 15, 1864. "Behind us lay Atlanta," its conqueror noted, "smoldering and in ruins, the black smoke rising high in the air, and hanging like a pall over the ruined city. . . . Then we turned our horses' heads to the east; Atlanta was soon lost behind the screen of trees and became a thing of the past."

In Special Field Orders No. 21, Sherman laid out the rules of engagement and sustenance for his troops. He wanted his army to march on parallel roads, heading east to points indicated by himself. This would spread his army out, covering some sixty miles. The cavalry would report directly to him. Brigadier General Judson Kilpatrick commanded this arm. "The army will forage liberally on the country," Sherman noted, an order that was later interpreted as giving a wide latitude, despite orders specifying that "each brigade commander will organize a good and

Maj. Gen. Henry Slocum was an active Democratic politician after the war and served several terms in Congress. (loc)

Maj. Gen. Judson Kilpatrick was a lightning rod for controversy. He was nicknamed "Kill Cavalry" for his habit of ordering suicidal charges. He was known to frequent prostitutes and was once arrested for drunkenness in Washington, D.C., during the war. (loc)

Tasked with supplying the army during the Savannah and Carolinas campaigns, Sherman's bummers developed a reputation for wanton violence and plunder. (loc)

sufficient foraging party, under the command of one or more discreet officers."

Prescribing a march of ten miles per day, Sherman calculated that this rate would allow for maximum destruction along the way. Indeed, no railroad—or even station—escaped intact in the army's path. Major James Connelly reported that "every 'Gin House' we pass is burned; every stack of fodder we can't carry along is burned; every barn filled with grain is destroyed; in fact everything that can be of use to the Rebels is either carried off by our foragers or set on fire and burned." The devastation and fleecing of the "bummers," as the foragers were dubbed, caused residents to spread the word to their neighbors of the approaching Union hordes, like a row of falling dominoes. This sowing of discord and terror unfolded exactly as Sherman intended.

Milledgeville, the Georgia state capital at that time, served as the first conversion point for the army wings. The citizens were on edge. "For every voice of calm reason there was another reciting a litany of horrors ascribed to the Yankee horde that was about to descend on the city." On November 22, the left-wing commander, Henry Slocum, entered the town and made his headquarters in the Milledgeville Hotel. Sherman rode into the capital the next day.

Arriving, the chieftain of the "Yankee horde" was amused by the flight of state authorities in advance of his army. He noted, "the people of Milledgeville remained at home, except the Governor [Brown], the

The Old Governor's Mansion in Milledgeville became Sherman's headquarters during the campaign to Savannah. While it had largely been stripped of furniture, Sherman simply used his camp equipment. (loc)

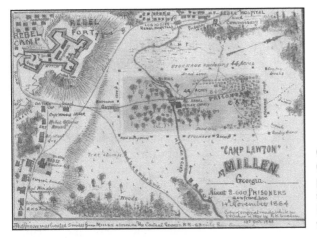

Camp Lawton near Millen, Georgia, was a short-lived prisoner of war camp holding some 10,000 Union soldiers. It existed for less than six weeks. (wc)

State Officers, and Legislature, who had ignominiously fled, in the utmost disorder and confusion." Slocum, who had arrived earlier, had seen to the security of the city and imposed order to Sherman's satisfaction. Making his headquarters at the Governor's mansion, he observed that the building "had hastily [been] stripped . . . of its carpets, curtains, and furniture . . . even the cabbages and vegetables from his kitchen and cellar" had been carried off.

According to orders, the Union Army destroyed everything of military value in Milledgeville, including an arsenal. Meanwhile, Sherman issued orders "for the next stage of the march as far as Millen. These were, substantially, for the right wing to follow the

This iconic print offers a melodramatic depiction of the devastation wrought by Sherman's soldiers on his famous March to the Sea. (loc)

Savannah Railroad, by roads on its south; the left wing was to move to Sandersville, by Davisboro and Louisville, while the cavalry was ordered by a circuit to the north, and to march rapidly for Millen, to rescue our prisoners of war confined there." Unfortunately, before Kilpatrick arrived, Confederate authorities evacuated the 10,000 Union prisoners at Camp Lawton.

About December 1, Sherman crossed over to the right wing and rode with Blair's corps. Howard was notified to move his wing along the Ogeechee River, preparatory to a move on Savannah. The soil grew increasingly sandy and the land marshy. Except for rice growing in roadside paddies, there would be little for the foragers to gather, unless they wished to tangle with alligators. Anticipating that Savannah would be fortified and garrisoned, which would slow progress during which time supplies would be used up, Sherman wanted to establish contact with the Union navy as soon as possible. As it turned out, they were looking for him, just as he sought them out.

Located on the Ogeechee River near Savannah, Georgia, Fort McAllister was an earthen fort that was part of the defenses of the city. The fort was inspected early in the war by Robert E. Lee, who suggested modifications that were then adopted. (loc)

The key to contacting the navy was control of the Ossabaw Sound below Savannah. But an old earthwork fort guarded the approach, preventing ships from steaming up. Fort McAllister would have to be taken. Aggressive as always, Kilpatrick volunteered for the job, but Sherman wanted infantry to storm the place. The job fell to Brig. Gen. William B. Hazen's Second Division, XV Corps.

Awaiting the assault, Sherman joined Howard atop an old rice mill about three miles opposite the fort. In his memoirs, the impatient commander recalled in detail his anticipation. "At that very moment," he recalled later, "some one discovered a ·faint cloud of smoke, and an object gliding . . . along the horizon. . . . which little by little grew till it was pronounced to be the smoke-stack of a steamer coming up the river. . . . Soon the flag of the United States was plainly visible." Still excited over the experience year later, the redheaded general remembered the following exchange. "Who are you?" the boat signaled.

"General Sherman," army signalmen answered. "Is Fort McAllister taken?" they asked. "Not yet," Sherman responded, "but it will be in a minute." Right on cue, Hazen's troops stormed the fort.

It took more than a minute to subdue the fort, but not a significant length of time. Blue troops swarmed over the parapet and overwhelmed the small garrison. Soon Sherman and Howard dined with Hazen near the fort, the former already making plans to drop downriver to find the fleet. After the meal and a quick tour of the fort, they set out. Six miles down, they found the *Dandelion*, a tender from the U.S. gunboat *Flag*. Contact established, Sherman sat down, penned letters to all necessary parties, and arranged to open the supply line to his army behind Savannah. Once the army had been refitted and resupplied, he would be ready to take the city.

Confederate Lt. Gen. William J. Hardee, a native of Georgia, commanded the Savannah defenses, a thankless task. Nearly surrounded by the U. S. Navy on the coast and sound and with Sherman's army at the western door, his only hope to avoid surrender and capture was to escape into South Carolina. But that posed dangers too. To effect his escape, he began work on a make-shift route island-hopping the Savannah River with jerry-rigged bridges.

Sherman, who had been on a visit to Rear Admiral Dahlgren aboard the USS *Harvest Moon*, returned on December 15 and established headquarters on the Plank Road near Howard. There he began making arrangements for placing of large guns in anticipation of a siege. Just then, a member of Grant's staff arrived and told Sherman to prepare his force to join him in Virginia. In this way, Grant asked Sherman to give up the capture of Savannah.

Disgruntled, Sherman determined that while preparing for the move by sea, he might still have time to gain the city. He told his chief that he preferred the overland route through the Carolinas, but had begun to arrange with the navy for the hundred or so vessels that would be needed to ferry his army to the Old Dominion. This was a tall order, since the navy had its hands full operating against the North Carolina coast with an assault on Fort Fisher in the making.

A subplot fueled Grant's anxiety and desire for Sherman to join him. Thomas was in Nashville, and Hood stood with his rebel army just outside the city. Yet Thomas did not attack. Grant had ordered the

Born in Vermont in 1830, Union Maj. Gen. William Babcock Hazen was a West Point graduate and regular army officer. After the war, he was an American observer in Europe during the Franco-Prussian War. (loc)

Rear Admiral John A. Dahlgren created the Bureau of Ordnance for the Union Navy during the Civil War and invented a cannon that would take his name. (loc)

ponderous loyalist Virginian to attack immediately, but
Thomas delayed, complaining about icy conditions.
Upset, Grant made plans to relieve Thomas if he did
not soon come out of Nashville and engage Hood.
Astonished to hear of this development, Sherman
wrote Grant, "I know full well that General Thomas
is slow in mind and in action; but he is judicious and
brave, and the troops feel great confidence in him. I
still hope he will outmaneuver and destroy Hood."
Thomas essentially did that on December 15–16,
wrecking Hood's army. With that pressure relieved,
Grant told Sherman to cancel the move to Virginia.

With Hardee nearly surrounded, Sherman tried
by letter to entice his surrender, only to be politely
declined. The Union commander determined to
cut off the rebel escape hatch and capture the entire
Confederate force. However, before this could be
completed, Hardee and his garrison escaped into
South Carolina. Sherman rode into the city on
December 22 and made his headquarters in the
mansion of an Englishman, Mr. Charles Green. Soon
after, on the suggestion of a U.S. Treasury agent who

Map of the siege and
investment of Savannah by
Union army artist Robert Knox
Sneden. (loc)

appeared to take possession of all confiscated cotton, the famous author of the "March to the Sea" penned a telegram addressed to Abraham Lincoln: "I beg to present you as a Christmas-gift the city of Savannah."

Known as the Green-Meldrim House today, this Savannah mansion became Maj. Gen. William Tecumseh Sherman's headquarters in December 1864 during the Union army's occupation. (loc)

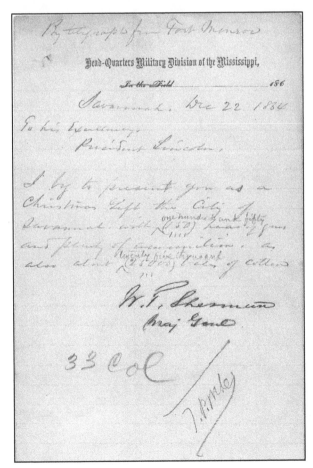

This telegram to President Lincoln offering Savannah as a Christmas gift was the result of a conversation between Sherman and a Federal Treasury agent in Savannah. (wc)

A Hero Betrayed

CHAPTER TEN
JANUARY 1865–APRIL 1865

A statue of Joe Johnston stands on the Bentonville battlefield, site of the largest clash of the Carolina campaign. Johnston's and Sherman's time against each other in Georgia and in the Carolinas gave them a mutual respect that, after the war, blossomed into friendship. Johnston eventually served as a pallbearer at Sherman's funeral. Although he stood in the rain during the service, Johnston uncovered his head out of respect. "If I were in his place, and he were standing here in mine, he would not put on his hat," he told someone. Johnston developed pneumonia as a result and died ten days later. (cm)

Immortalized in song and remembered as one of the iconic moments in the American Civil War, Sherman's March to the Sea seared itself into American memory and perhaps the Southern psyche. "So too did Sherman come to be the ultimate personification of those evils," wrote historian Anne Sarah Rubin, "If the marchers were 'Huns' or 'Vandals,' then Sherman was Attila; if the March was one long arson spree, then Sherman was Nero incarnate."

In his memoirs, the aging general later reflected on the public perception versus his intent regarding his Savannah Campaign. "Still, then, as now, the march to the sea was generally regarded as something extraordinary, something anomalous, something out of the usual order of events; whereas, in fact, I simply moved from Atlanta to Savannah, as one step in the direction of Richmond, a movement that had to be met and defeated, or the war was necessarily at an end." Modeling the becoming modesty of the hero, Sherman penned this remembrance when his legacy was secure. But, in the moment, he enjoyed the accolades that rained down on him.

Grant, still stalled in front of Petersburg, felt relieved that Sherman and his army had reappeared on the coast after a deafening silence. "I never had a doubt of the result," the General-in-Chief wrote Sherman. "When apprehensions for your safety were expressed by the President, I assured him with the army you had, and you in command of it, there was

Print of Sherman's troops entering Savannah at the conclusion of their march across Georgia. Once rested and resupplied the army would swing north through the Carolinas. (loc)

no danger but you would *strike* bottom on salt-water some place; that I would not feel the same security—in fact, would not have entrusted the expedition to any other living commander."

"Our Military Santa Claus," as the *Chicago Tribune* dubbed him, enjoyed a sumptuous Christmas dinner at the Green mansion with his staff. After attending church service at St. John's Episcopal Church near his headquarters, Sherman and his staff attended to army matters until the evening, when about 20 officers, plus Mr. Green, gathered around the table to enjoy roast turkey, "a splendid chicken pie, cold slaw, celery, sweet potatoes, turnips, champagne" and many assorted desserts.

Sherman and his army passed a pleasant Christmas season in Savannah. Letters, some private and many official, flew from the army headquarters. Sherman's mind had already turned to planning his next steps. Grant had relented about bringing the redhead's army by sea to Virginia. Instead, a campaign through the Carolinas lay in the planning stage. The army targeted South Carolina with particular wrath. "The truth is the whole army is burning with an insatiable desire to wreak vengeance upon South Carolina," Sherman told Halleck. "I almost tremble at her fate, but feel she deserves all that seems in store for her."

Despite his brother Senator John Sherman's assurance that Secretary of War Edwin Stanton held a favorable opinion of him, General Sherman was unsettled by Stanton's unannounced visit to Savannah in January 1865. With his army recuperating from its 300-mile adventure marching to the sea, Sherman busily focused on resupplying his army and planning for a campaign into the Carolinas. The surprise appearance of the Secretary of War not only promised to interfere with these preparations but also to portend trouble.

In his memoirs, Sherman recalled Stanton's visit. "He talked to me a great deal about the negroes," the general wrote. "He inquired particularly about Major General Jeff C. Davis, who, he said, was a Democrat, and hostile to the negro." Stanton had heard about the incident involving Davis, commander of the XIV Corps, and the many African Americans following the army at Ebenezer Creek. As the army had approached Savannah, Davis, who regarded the freedmen as a burden, saw an opportunity to lose them. When his men had crossed Ebenezer Creek, he ordered the pontoon bridge cut and pulled back before the freedmen could cross, effectively leaving them stranded on the far side as Davis and his men moved on. As Sherman remembered it, Stanton "showed me a newspaper account of General Davis taking up his pontoon bridge . . . leaving sleeping negro men, women, and children, on the other side, to be slaughtered by Wheeler's cavalry."

Sherman suggested an interview with Davis to clear up the matter, and Stanton agreed. Subsequently, at the interview, Davis "explained the matter to [Stanton's] entire satisfaction," according to Sherman's recollection. Years later, the still irritated general noted that "General Jeff. C. Davis was strictly a soldier, and doubtless hated to have his wagons and columns encumbered by these poor negroes, for whom we all felt sympathy, but sympathy of a different sort from that of Mr. Stanton, which was not of pure humanity, but of politics." Written many years after the war, the scorn reflected in these words not only reflects Sherman's disdain of bureaucrats in general, but a powerful disregard for Stanton borne out of a later controversy over the terms of surrender Sherman initially offered Confederate Gen. Joe Johnston in April 1865.

Stanton continued his visit, meeting with African American ministers from the Savannah area. During part of this interview, the secretary of war asked Sherman to leave the room so Stanton could get an unvarnished answer to what they thought of the general. Although the answers given to Stanton offered

Union Maj. Gen. (brevet) Jefferson C. Davis was a hot-tempered but competent commander who was known for killing General William Nelson following an argument in Kentucky in 1862. Interestingly, Davis was never tried for the murder of his superior officer. (loc)

In a pencil sketch by artist William Waud, General Sherman is seen reviewing his troops in Savannah. (loc)

a glowing tribute to Sherman, as he later discovered, the general was undoubtedly furious over the matter. "It certainly was a strange fact," Sherman wrote in his memoirs, "that the great War Secretary should have catechized negroes concerning the character of a general who had commanded a hundred thousand men in battle, had captured cities, conducted sixty-five thousand men successfully across four hundred miles of hostile territory, and had just brought tens of thousands of freedmen to a place of security."

While Stanton's visit to Savannah seemed to store up trouble for the future, it also brought about Sherman's famous Special Field Orders No. 15. Before he went north again, Stanton wanted some assurance that the freedmen following Sherman's army would be provided for. The plan they worked out would later be characterized as providing "Forty Acres and a Mule." Confiscated lands off the coast of Georgia and South Carolina—the Sea Isles—would be parceled out to freedmen who could then cultivate the land without the interference of any whites, who were prohibited from visiting the Isles. "It was a revolutionary document," according to historian John F. Marszalek, "and it is ironic that someone with Sherman's antiblack attitudes should have issued it." Of course, though the orders were Sherman's, the sentiment was not.

Doubtless, Sherman breathed a sigh of relief when Stanton departed Savannah on January 15, heading north. Though he and Stanton got on well socially, Sherman had learned to be a bit wary of the secretary. More than anything else, what the general wanted was to "get into the pine-woods again, free from the importunities of rebel women asking for protection, and of the civilians from the North who were coming to Savannah for cotton and all sorts of profit." He was ready to take his army into South Carolina.

By the middle of January, Sherman was burning with a desire to be off. While the Atlanta and Savannah campaigns had been exhausting, he did not want to sit and wait. He believed that Confederate morale was low and their will to continue the fight was eroding fast. He didn't want to give them time to recover. "My aim then was, to whip the rebels," the Ohioan wrote years later, "to humble their pride, to follow them to their inmost recesses, and make them fear and dread us."

When the army moved out of Savannah on January 21, the people of Charleston waited, petrified that they were about to feel the wrath of the Union hordes. The birthplace of secession, Halleck hoped, would receive special attention. "Should you capture Charleston," the Army Chief of Staff wrote Sherman, "I hope that by some accident the place may be destroyed, and, if a little salt should be sown upon its site, it may prevent the growth of future crops of nullification and secession."

Sherman had long since decided to bypass Charleston, though he did enjoy making enough of a demonstration to scare the daylights out of the residents who had not already fled. "It was manifest to me," the Union hero wrote, "that the soldiers and the people of the South entertained an undue fear of our Western men, and, like children, they had invented such ghostlike stories of our prowess in Georgia, that they were scared by their own inventions. Still, this was a power, and I intended to utilize it."

Miserable weather descended as the army set out into the Palmetto State. Delays were unavoidable as localized flooding made roads almost impassable. Finally, in early February, things began to improve. Though still cold, the rains ceased, and the work of destruction began in earnest.

On Valentine's Day, Sherman informed his commanders that their immediate destination would be Columbia, the capital of South Carolina. Meanwhile, he kept up diversions to keep the Confederates guessing about his intentions. The cavalry had feinted at Augusta and baffled Confederate authorities. As the army approached Columbia, only Confederate General Wade Hampton's cavalry guarded the town, and they were soon driven off.

A wild scene greeted Sherman as he rode into the state capital city. Cotton bales lined the streets; some torn open with lint flying everywhere, others on fire. Looting had preceded his arrival with the result that the streets were littered with wreckage. Drunken Union soldiers, plied with liquor by grateful slaves, greeted the army commander with song and jibes. According to Marszalek, "Black reaction was even more exuberant. Slaves ran after Sherman, yelling, and dancing, and clapping and loudly thanking God for his arrival."

Sherman tasked Howard with bringing order to the chaotic city. Union authorities were besieged

Columbia was the capital of South Carolina during the Civil War. During the colonial period the location featured a frontier fort and fur trading post on the banks of the Congaree River. (nypl)

with requests to protect private property. After touring Columbia, Sherman issued the necessary orders to destroy everything of military value to the Confederacy and retired to his headquarters a few blocks from the capitol.

Awakened from a well-deserved slumber that night, Sherman arose to find a city in more turmoil. The city was ablaze, fueled by drifting cotton, intoxicated soldiers, and revenge-minded skulkers. Turning out to help fight the fires, the Union commander entered a nightmare. Gale force winds whipped the flames quicker than firefighters could douse them, creating a losing fight. By morning, more than a third of Columbia lay in ashes. "Sherman wasn't sorry, nor would he ever be," historian Robert L. O'Connell wrote. "On the plane he was now waging war, it had been the climactic moment in his horror show for Southern edification, and he later claimed it was the death-blow for the rebellion."

For his part, Sherman declined the blame. "Though I never ordered it and never wished it, I have never shed many tears over the event, because I believe it hastened what we all fought for, the end of the war." The fires were the work of Hampton's cavalry, whiskey, and the wind, but, in the end, just another incident of war.

By early March, the Union army crossed into North Carolina. Here, Sherman wanted to wield the velvet glove and not the iron fist. "Every effort will be made," Slocum told his troops, "To prevent any wanton destruction of property, or any unkind treatment of citizens." Of course, the soldiers viewed North Carolina differently than its southern neighbor, not being marred with the stench of treason. Besides this, they already knew that a strong peace movement existed here, which called for a different approach. The matches were stowed away.

Joe Johnston's presence fueled yet another consideration in North Carolina. Returned to command of his old army, largely because Jefferson Davis had no other choice, Johnston now lay between Sherman and Goldsboro, where he planned to rest, refit, and gather reinforcements. Laying a trap at Bentonville, Sherman's old nemesis tried to isolate Davis's Union corps, which led to the only significant battle of the campaign, March 19–21. But when

Sherman brought up reinforcements, Johnston wisely withdrew.

Reaching Goldsboro, Sherman met Schofield's XXIII Corps and two divisions under the command of Maj. Gen. Alfred Terry soon joined to bring the combined strength of the Union force above 90,000. Johnston's numbers were far too weak to dare attack Sherman now. He waited and watched instead. Jefferson Davis, as always, wanted boldness, but by now was resigned to Johnston's caution.

With the army secured in its camps; Sherman decided to leave Schofield in command so he could run up to City Point to see Grant. It had been over a year since they last met. The reunion gratified the old chums, who enjoyed swapping stories about their exploits. Sherman, of course, did most of the talking. Lincoln was on hand too, as it turned out, on holiday from Washington. The day after Sherman arrived, a high-level meeting convened on Lincoln's boat, *The River Queen*. Grant and Sherman represented the army and Admiral David Porter the navy. Much of the conversation revolved around the war's end, which loomed plainly in sight. "He wanted peace on almost any terms," Porter recalled the president saying. "His heart was tenderness throughout, and as long as the rebels laid down their arms, he did not care how it was done."

Sherman left much affected by the *River Queen* conference. He formed a higher opinion of Lincoln than ever. The president's desire for peace and his wishes for how to bring it about gave him a clear idea of what kind of terms to offer, should he be able to offer them in North Carolina. "I never saw him again," Sherman later wrote in his memoir. "Of all the men I ever met, he seemed to possess more of the elements of greatness, combined with goodness, than any other."

Grant and Sherman, among other things, had set a schedule and a general plan for the spring campaign during their visit in City Point. Arriving back at Goldsboro, the voluble commander set to work preparing the army for what he believed to be the closing chapter of the war. He reorganized the army into three wings: Howard with the Army of the Tennessee, Schofield with the Army of the Ohio, and Slocum commanding the newly styled Army of Georgia. They were to move promptly against Johnston on April 10. Grant, meanwhile, promised to

Union Maj. Gen. Alfred Terry was a graduate of Yale Law School. At the start of the war, Terry was colonel of the 2nd Connecticut Infantry. (loc)

The battle of Bentonville, March 1865, was the last meaningful battle of the Civil War—and the largest battle fought in North Carolina. (cm)

break Lee's line around Petersburg. On the off chance that Lee got away from Grant and sought a junction with Johnston, Sherman had assured his chief that his army could hold against the combination until the Army of the Potomac arrived.

However, before Sherman's preparations advanced too far, word reached Goldsboro that Grant had broken Lee's line. The depleted Army of Northern Virginia then rushed westward, trying to escape capture. Richmond had fallen, and Jefferson Davis hurried south. Better be ready, Grant advised Sherman: should Lee escape Virginia, "you will have to take care of him." Not to worry, the excited redhead assured his chief. "You have established a reputation for perseverance and pluck that would make Wellington jump out of his coffin."

Lee surrendered to Grant on April 9, 1865, at a roadside hamlet called Appomattox Court House. On April 12, Sherman announced the news to an exuberant army. He hoped that his turn to offer terms to Joe Johnston would soon come. Little did he know, though, that dissension filled the ranks of Confederate authorities. Davis, in denial, vowed to raise legions and continue the war. Declaring this madness, Johnston promised to meet Sherman and pursue peace. Davis continued to flee, casting aspersions left and right.

Johnston arranged to meet with Sherman on April 17 for a conference. When they met at a little farm owned by the Bennett family not far from Raleigh, both men carried a secret. Johnston could muster less than 15,000 men in his army that should have boasted 73,000. Sherman's news was darker. Just that morning, he had been notified that Lincoln had been assassinated. Once alone, Sherman handed Johnston the telegram which had announced the murder of Lincoln. Blanching, Johnston stuttered unbelievingly that "Mr. Lincoln was the best friend they had" and that the news was "the greatest possible calamity to the South."

Two days of conferences finally produced terms that, in the words of Robert L. O'Connell, "was a sweetheart of a deal" for the Confederates. Joined by Confederate Secretary of War John Breckinridge on the second day, the former U.S. vice president talked Sherman into terms encompassing both military and civil. "Confederate armies were to deposit their weapons at arsenals located in their own capitals. Existing state governments were to be recognized once they swore a loyalty oath and Federal courts

Robert E. Lee's surrender to U.S. Grant at Appomattox Court House, Virginia. The surrender occurred in the parlor of the home of William McLean. (loc)

Home of James Bennett and family, Bennett Place became the site of Confederate General Joe Johnston's surrender to Union general William Tecumseh Sherman. One of James Bennett's sons, Lorenzo, served in the war in the 27th North Carolina Infantry. (loc)

reestablished. The political rights of all individuals in seceding states were guaranteed, and no one would be punished . . . as long as they maintained the peace." Believing that Lincoln had given him permission to extend such terms, Sherman confidently believed this would finish the job of ending the war. But he was mistaken, and the blowback followed nearly immediately.

Stanton furiously accused Sherman of colluding with Jefferson Davis. President Andrew Johnson wanted the thing done and sent Grant to secure Johnston's surrender on identical terms offered to Lee. Grant appeared unannounced at Sherman's headquarters and quietly told him to return to Johnston and finish the job with terms acceptable to Washington. This was done on April 26, and the war essentially ended.

Surprised by Grant's appearance, Sherman quietly followed his orders, unaware that a storm of

This print depicts a meeting between Sherman and General Johnston at the time of the latter's surrender. (loc)

Shot at close range by actor John Wilkes Booth in Ford's Theater, President Lincoln died the following morning at 7:22 a.m. in the Peterson House across the street from the theater. (loc)

controversy was already swirling about him. Assigning the actual formalities of surrender to subordinate officers, the redhead was ready to move on with his other duties—even as the dark clouds rolled in.

Vice President under Abraham Lincoln, Andrew Johnson became the 17th President of the United States upon Lincoln's death. Johnson spent most of the war as the Military Governor of Tennessee. (loc)

Securing a Legacy

CHAPTER ELEVEN

APRIL 1865–FEBRUARY 1891

With the surrenders of Lee and Johnston, the long national nightmare neared its end. However, for Sherman, this did not mean an end to feuds, both political and personal. At a time when he might be expected to joyously celebrate the end of the four-year fraternal blood bath, a controversy riveted his attention, stemming from the terms he had offered Johnston before being overruled in Washington.

Stanton angrily complained that Sherman had thrown "away all the advantages we had gained from the war." As he often did, Stanton repeated his bitter tirade against Sherman to anyone who would listen. Halleck, now in charge of Richmond, dealt in rumor, suggesting perhaps that Davis and Sherman were in cahoots with Confederate treasury money greasing the skids.

At first ignorant of the charges being leveled against him from on high, the Ohioan soon learned when the newspapers, undoubtedly at Stanton's suggestion, took up the controversy. "When Stanton branded Sherman a traitor and threat to the Union," historian Marszalek later wrote, "the slur found receptive ears." Soon the old charge of insanity returned. Once again, the press willingly amplified it. Years later, Sherman still chafed, "To say that I was angry . . . would hardly express the state of my feelings. I was outraged beyond measure, and was resolved to resent the insult, cost what it might."

Like America itself, Sherman's heart looked westward after the Civil War. St. Louis would become his literal and spiritual home, and he would eventually be buried there. (cm)

Halleck, trying to curry favor in Washington, made a serious mistake by joining the chorus of accusations against his old friend. Sherman had spent the whole war professing the most heartfelt gratitude to "Old Brains" for his help in saving his career. Learning that Halleck had wired his subordinate commanders and instructed them not to obey his orders was a bridge too far. A passionate man, Sherman loved whole-heartedly but could hate unforgivingly. Halleck now resided in the latter category and lost a loyal friend who would soon be in a position to help those he admired.

Sherman and his armies marched for Washington, where Eastern and Western forces participated in a Grand Review on May 23 and 24, passing before President Johnson and assembled dignitaries. It was a great pageant, and anticipation simmered in Washington. Flags, buntings, and all manner of patriotic displays livened the scene. The main attraction—the soldiers themselves—marched splendidly. Amid the celebration, Sherman gained a small measure of revenge. After passing in review, he was invited to join the assembled VIPs on the viewing stand. There, he shook hands with Johnson, Grant, and other cabinet members. When he got to Stanton, and the secretary offered his hand, the still-irate general just glared—refusing to shake hands. Everyone nearby noticed the slight.

On May 30, Sherman issued farewell orders to the Military Division of the Mississippi. "The general commanding announces to the Armies of Tennessee and Georgia that the time has come for us to part," he began.

Erected near the White House, a large reviewing stand was constructed for VIPs to watch the two-day Grand Review of Union armies. (loc)

Our work is done, and armed enemies no longer defy us. . . . Your general now bids you farewell, with the full belief that, as in war you have been good soldiers, so in peace you will make good citizens; and if, unfortunately, new war should arise in our country, "Sherman's army" will be the first to buckle on its old armor and come forth to defend and maintain the Government of our inheritance.

This 1885 photo of an aged General William Tecumseh Sherman is notable for the epaulets he very rarely wore. The photo was taken to mark Sherman's retirement as commanding general of U.S. armies. (wc)

While the celebrations in Washington had been a pleasant interlude, Sherman anxiously wanted to get out of the nest of vipers he so despised in the capital. John might thrive in that atmosphere, but his hero brother longed to breathe western air. In June, new orders confirmed that the redhead would continue to command the Military Division of the Mississippi, which extended to the Rocky Mountains and stretched from the Northern border to the Southern. Besides his normal duties, he was expected to oversee the completion of the Transcontinental Railroad. His headquarters would be in St. Louis, which no doubt pleased him. Promotion to lieutenant general came in July 1866; Grant received the appointment at the same time to General of the Army.

Always a restless spirit, Sherman continued to travel extensively, touring every corner of his division. The question of Western expansion ranked high in his mind along with those he saw as the obstacles to that progress—Native Americans. "We must act with vindictive earnestness against the Sioux, even to their extermination, men, women and children," the lanky general wrote Grant. "Nothing else will reach the roots of this case."

Perhaps he exaggerated, but there is little doubt that Sherman wanted to subjugate Native Americans. In fact, he even devised a way to do just that—eliminate the primary food supply: buffalo. "To say Sherman encouraged buffalo hunting completely understates the case," biographer Robert L. O'Connell observed in *Fierce Patriot*. "He declared war on them, orchestrating the killing of roughly 5,000,000 beasts between 1867 and 1874." This strategy was pursued without mercy and would be highly effective.

In November 1868, Ulysses S. Grant was elected president. As expected, Sherman became General of the Army. This, as it turned out, led to a long period of frustration and political turmoil. Power struggles with Secretaries of War, including Grant's former

President Ulysses S. Grant was elected the 18th President of the United States in 1868. His two terms were riveted with scandal—though Grant himself was scrupulously honest. (loc)

Sherman and U.S. Commissioners negotiated a treaty with the Sioux and Arapaho tribes at Fort Laramie, Wyoming, in 1868. (wc)

chief of staff John Rawlins and later William Belknap, reduced the power of the commanding general. In 1870, John A. Logan, the famous "Black Jack," now a congressman, found an opportunity to settle an old score with Sherman by introducing a bill in Congress to cut the military budget by $2,000,000 and the salary of the General of the Army by nearly $20,000. Efforts to squash the bill largely failed.

In October 1871, the Ewing family patriarch, Thomas, died. His formal conversion to Catholicism comforted his family, especially Ellen. Sherman, for his part, had mixed feelings. Part of him always appreciated Ewing for taking him in and all the support, but he also resented his interference in his family life.

Ewing's passing also marked the beginning of a serious decline in Sherman's marriage to Ellen. As always, differences over religion were at the heart of the problems. Her father's conversion "encouraged her to expect rather than to hope that Sherman would follow suit," biographer Brian Holden Reid observed. "Her less than subtle efforts would grate and provoke. [But] the wall of Sherman's agnosticism proved impenetrable."

This now-iconic photograph shows thousands of bison skulls about to be ground up for fertilizer in Detroit, Michigan. The circa 1892 photo has been used to illustrate the destruction of the American bison in the 19th century. In 1800, there were approximately 50 million buffalo roaming the Great Plains. One hundred years later, fewer than 500 remained. (wc)

A ten-month trip abroad gave Sherman time to reflect and escape. Leaving Ellen at home, he traveled with Grant's son, Fred, and some staff officers. The largely military-themed trip first took him to Spain, France, and Italy. In Rome, he secured an audience with the Pope, which must have pleased his wife. From there, he moved on to Egypt, Constantinople, and

LEFT: **A graduate of Princeton University, William W. Belknap became secretary of war under President Grant. He resigned in 1876 following a scandal.** (loc)

RIGHT: **Secretary of War John A. Rawlins served on the staff of Ulysses S. Grant throughout the Civil War, rising in rank to major general (by brevet). Rawlins died just months into his tenure at the War Department.** (loc)

Sevastopol, where he visited the siege lines. Moscow, St. Petersburg, Berlin, and Zurich, Switzerland came next. The trip finally made a tour of the United Kingdom, with visits to London, Edinburgh, and Dublin. A high point was an invitation to have an audience with Queen Victorian at her home on the Isle of Wight.

Sherman arrived home in time to see Grant reelected president. His opponent, Horace Greeley, the ambitious editor of the *New York Tribune* who had vexed Lincoln, would have made, according to the commanding general, "the worst president any country ever had." Apart from the election, little had changed in Washington or the War Department.

To escape the political minefields of the capital, Sherman moved his headquarters to St. Louis in hopes of more peaceful days. But peace remained elusive. Soon, the general faced one of the great personal crises of his life. He discovered that his son, Tom, had committed to becoming a Catholic priest. While this decision, of course, delighted Ellen, Sherman was devastated. It was a dark time for the despondent father, who now told a friend that he regarded his son "as dead." He was furious at Ellen, who had encouraged Tom's ambitions and the church, which he ranked as "one of our public enemies."

Troubled, Sherman continued to wander, avoiding contact with Ellen. He moved his headquarters back to Washington and continued to travel extensively. Over the winter of 1879, the general even visited Atlanta and traced his path to Savannah with daughter Lizzie in tow. "In not a single instance was a word uttered that was rude, impolite or offensive," Sherman recalled.

New Hampshire-born Horace Greeley was an advocate for a general movement westward. He was known for his slogan, "Go West, young man." (loc)

Father Thomas Ewing
Sherman was the second
son of William Tecumseh and
Ellen Ewing Sherman. Born
in San Francisco, California,
Tom disappointed his father
by becoming a Catholic priest.
(wc)

Sherman, even as an older man, was a flirt, and it is natural to wonder if the general was always faithful. Certainly, the impassioned old general had many female admirers, especially after the war. Emotionally and physically separated from Ellen, as he often was, a dalliance may have provided some comfort. There is no positive evidence of an affair, though biographer Michael Fellman contends that Mary Audenried, widow of Sherman's long-time aide, "took him to her bed."

On November 1, 1883, Sherman turned over command of the Army to Philip Sheridan and retired to St. Louis with full pay and benefits for life. That should have ended his public life, but in the presidential election cycle of 1884, a strong movement emerged to put the old general in the White House. Even his brother, a perennial candidate himself, piled on. There were appeals to duty and patriotism to try to move the graying warrior. "I will not in any event entertain or accept a nomination," Sherman protested. "Patriotism does not demand of me what I construe as a sacrifice of judgement, of inclination and of self-interest."

The publication and reprintings of his memoirs occupied Sherman's mind over many years. Probably begun shortly after the war, according to historian Lee Kennett, Sherman "had a complete draft by early 1872." Contracting with the Appleton publishing company, the voluble commander wrote a friend, "I have just done a thing that I may regret all my life." He had committed to publishing his memoirs but seemed to know it would cause controversy.

What motivated Sherman to write and publish his memoirs is not too difficult to discern. Though he never recorded his thoughts on this specifically, he did seem to have the "rising generation" in mind. To them, he wished they would learn from his recollections "that a country and government such as ours are worth fighting for, and dying for, if need be." One thing is clear: the conqueror of Atlanta believed that reliable histories of the war needed to be written by Union men. Writing to a former member of his military staff, Willard Warner, Sherman argued, "We the victors must stamp on all history that we were right and they were wrong—that we beat them in battle as well as in argument."

It is also possible that the Ohio general chafed at the slow progress of the compilation of the Official

Records, which he lamented, "probable that a new century will come before they are published and circulated." This being so, Sherman wanted to ensure that he recorded his "recollection of events" to "account for the motives and reasons which influenced some of the actors in the grand drama of war." Although he wrote of "some of the actors" — plural—what he meant was that he wanted to explain HIS motives and reasons before someone else did. Since he could not have the last word, he would have the first.

The publication of Grant's memoirs, after the old general's death in 1885 from throat cancer, pleased Sherman greatly. Although the two men had grown apart and the friendship had cooled significantly, he still admired his old chief and felt that Grant's recollections went far to sustain his own version of events. Phil Sheridan died in 1888, and George Thomas had died back in 1870. His comrades were dying around him, and Cump probably felt isolated. Then, at the end of November 1888, Ellen passed away. Her death was surprisingly hard on Sherman, who had rushed to her deathbed saying, "Wait for me, Ellen—no one ever loved you as I loved you."

In 1890, Sherman turned seventy. He increasingly talked of his own mortality. "I feel death reaching out for me," he told a friend. Still, he continued to enjoy company, public and private dinners, and the theater. After an outing in February 1891, the old warrior came down with a staph infection which caused a fever. Asthma complicated the ailment, and the physicians

Phillip Sheridan as commanding general of the U.S. Army. Present in Chicago during the Great Chicago Fire in 1871, Sheridan was briefly in charge of the city when martial law was declared, and the mayor deferred to the old hero. (loc)

This rare Sherman family photo features not only the aging general, but his equally famous brother John as well. (ms)

Sherman's post-war home in Washington, D.C. While he spent plenty of time in the capital, the general strongly disliked the atmosphere. (wc)

A common 19th century practice was the creation of a death mask for prominent men. (pd)

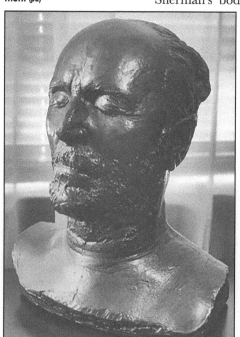

grew worried. The family began to gather. Pneumonia settled into Sherman's chest, and he passed in and out of consciousness. On February 11, the Sherman clan had a Catholic priest administer last rites—something the wizened old general would have protested. Finally, on Sunday, February 14, just before 2:00 p.m., the last embers of Sherman's fire went cold.

While final arrangements were being made, Sherman's body was viewed by thousands in New York. "Undertakers dressed him in his general's uniform with its yellow sash across his breast," Lloyd Lewis wrote. "Seven tapers in a brass candelabrum threw soft light on the nose that still curved like a cutlass. . . . Except for the whitening of his beard, he looked almost younger than at forty. On the coffin lay his soldier's cap and sword."

At his request, the general's bones were laid beside his son Willie in Cavalry Cemetery, St. Louis. The inscription on the stone, requested by the general, reads "Faithful and honorable." A fitting testament to the old soldier, the gravestone is adorned with detailed flags and appropriate symbols—including a cartridge box marked "40 rounds."

Sherman's grave in Calvary Cemetery in St. Louis lies near his beloved son Willie, who died of Typhoid Fever during the Civil War. (ddm)

While tributes to the old warrior would fill volumes, perhaps the most fitting was penned by General O. O. Howard, who commanded a wing of Sherman's army during his famous March to the Sea. "In his heart was a love of truth, a phenomenal loyalty to his country, a fearless and prompt devotion to duty and markedly an absence of aught that was malicious. True, he resented wrong often with a fiery indignation, but he forgave a fault confessed with quick generosity."

General Sherman's stately St. Louis home stood at 912 Garrison Avenue, but no longer exists. In the early 20th century, it was divided into apartments. (ms)

Conclusion

CHAPTER TWELVE
LIKE A PHOENIX

A complex man, William Tecumseh Sherman never stopped searching for who he was. Even close to death, he sought to define himself. "Faithful and honorable," he repeatedly said as he neared the end, "faithful and honorable." Those are the words inscribed on his tombstone.

Tension defined his private life. He lived with the Ewings in Lancaster from age nine as a quasi-adopted son, while his mother lived just down the hill. He loved Thomas Ewing, his honorary father figure but also resented him. He desperately wanted his approval yet also wanted to be his own man. Sherman was a soldier who reluctantly became a civilian. His restless soul could not remain in one place. He married his quasi-sister Ellen, with whom he lived with for only a third of his married life. As an agnostic, he was chased, chastised, and badgered to become a Catholic. The general commanded the U.S. Army but sometimes had to conform to orders issued by the War Department. He was a hero, and he was a barbarian.

At his core, Sherman was a soldier and always would be. But finding his place—his niche—eluded him for a long time. He was an artilleryman, an inquisitor, and an administrator in his early career. As a civilian, he worked as a banker, a lawyer, an academy superintendent, and president of a streetcar company. At each step, the reflective redhead wondered, "Who am I?" He felt like a failure and was seemingly adrift.

The lion in winter: the Sherman statue in Manhattan's Grand Army Plaza. (wc/kh)

This 1866 portrait by George Peter Alexander Healy depicts General Sherman at the height of his fame. (wc)

The Civil War gave Sherman new life but also nearly destroyed him. From the start, he could have been a general but wanted to feel like he earned it and settled for a colonelcy. In his first battle, the Union army performed well at the start but faltered and ran. Later, Sherman did better than many and kept his men together and orderly. Promotion came unbidden and, in his mind, unearned. Then came Kentucky.

The insanity episode would have destroyed most people. It would have been easy to return to Lancaster and retire to private life. But the republic's fate was at stake, and Sherman was too restless and ambitious to abide retirement. He felt a burning desire to prove himself to Thomas Ewing, to Union authorities, to the public, but most of all, to himself.

Stress and anxiety got the better of the redhead, who was not ready for command and found himself thrust into a situation far from ideal. When he tried to alert Union authorities to the dangers, they disregarded him. When he told the Secretary of War what would be required to defend the Mississippi Valley, his sanity was questioned. Later, the newspapers declared him insane. He was ill, and he was utterly humiliated. But, like a phoenix, he rose from the ashes.

Two important developments began the process of rehabilitation and redefinition of Sherman. The first: his relationship with Grant. The second: the battle of Shiloh. The fellow Ohioan attached himself to the reticent general and never looked back. Grant inspired him, giving him a confidence in success. Shiloh demonstrated that Sherman could lead men in battle competently. Far from insane, the fiery general was cool and collected amid chaos.

By the time Sherman set out on the Atlanta Campaign in 1864, he stood confident and self-assured. Gone was the self-doubt and anxiety. In a years' time, he had risen from divisional command to lead the Army of the Tennessee to the leadership of the Military Division of the Mississippi and ultimately commanded an army group.

The capture of Atlanta solidified Sherman's place as a Union hero. The same people and papers that had ridiculed him back in Kentucky sung his praises and toasted his health. He was a victor in his own right and by his own design. With confidence came new notions of war. When he proposed the March to the Sea, Sherman told Grant, "This may not be war, but rather statesmanship."

Nothing fired the public imagination the way the March to the Sea did. Of course, the tantalizing silence while the army was out of contact and the speculation of the papers added to the mystery. Sherman thoroughly enjoyed the freedom of the march and the grand design he orchestrated. Later, in his memoirs, the general disingenuously downplayed the significance of the march. While many "regarded [the march] as something extraordinary, something anomalous, something out of the usual order of event," Sherman regarded it simply as a change of base. It was "a means to an end, and not . . . an essential act of war."

When Secretary Thomas Ewing died in 1871, then Governor (and later President) Rutherford B. Hayes was a pallbearer at his funeral. (pd)

Gratifyingly, plaudits flooded in during the Savannah interlude. Sherman's reputation blazed at its height—rivaling Grant's. There were even conversations about placing Sherman above his friend. "I don't want promotion, but on the contrary, I want rest, as soon as I can ask for it decently," he wrote his brother Senator John Sherman. "The law cannot confer military fame nor can it make my right to command greater than it now is. I have all the power that can possible be exercised. . . . When the war is over there will be time enough for honors and pensions, but now every possible pretext for jealousy and envy should be avoided." The country did not need another lieutenant general. "I would rather have you in command than anybody for you are fair, honest, and have at heart the same purpose that should animate all," Sherman wrote Grant. "I should emphatically decline any commission calculated to bring us into rivalry."

While the campaign through the Carolinas did little to alter the public perception of Sherman, the destruction in South Carolina did please many. The controversy over the terms of surrender offered to Johnston threatened to douse everything. It did not and could not change the soldiers' devotion to their "Uncle Billy," but newspaper accounts revived old insanity charges that left the general burning with fury. Much of Sherman's ire was aimed at Stanton, who hysterically accused him of treason, and Halleck, who suggested that he might have been bribed by Jefferson Davis.

Indeed, Sherman's brother staged interventions to cool the redhead's fierce temper—lest he do something so rash that his reputation would be wrecked. In the end, snubbing Halleck and Stanton allowed the general to gain a measure of satisfaction.

Eleanor Boyle Ewing
Sherman, wife of General
Sherman, predeceased her
husband in 1888 and is buried
in Calvary Cemetery, St. Louis.
(loc)

Still, the episode unnerved Sherman, who felt that the terms offered were what Lincoln had suggested. And, of course, he was deeply disturbed by the assassination itself.

The end of the war, predictably left Sherman feeling a bit adrift. He would have a long post-war life that pulled him increasingly into politics, which he loathed. He watched in horror as politics pulled Grant in all directions and then placed him in the White House. Part of Sherman thought that Grant's presidency, if nothing else, would be good for the army. In this, he was disappointed.

Sherman was promoted to General of the Army but still groped about for meaning and identity. He moved from place to place—Washington to St. Louis and back to Washington. He traveled extensively, reveling at least in his reception as a Union hero. Reunions of his veterans helped Sherman to relive his wartime glory. But an emptiness followed Sherman in the post-war world.

Nothing caused more despair for the old warrior than his family. To be sure, Sherman loved his children and enjoyed time with them, but the lowest moments were often connected to family affairs. His troubled marriage to Ellen fueled much of the general's travel to escape. Her increasingly strident attempts to bring him fully into the Catholic fold—especially after her father's death—frustrated Sherman, who grew increasingly estranged. But the discovery that his son, Tom, joined the Jesuit order led to such anguish that the general emotionally disowned his son and would not speak to his wife, whom he saw as responsible. These issues caused Sherman to question his role in the family.

Sherman was ebullient, and he was haunted. Fear of failure was a frequent companion. His cynicism could be well founded, though at times heavy-handed. A highly social animal, the general could also be a loner. This battle-scarred hero of the republic may have secured a place in history but spent much of his life in a quest to define himself. That he would be one of the first high-ranking officers on either side to write his memoirs is not surprising. More than wanting his version of the history of the war to be appreciated, he wanted to be the first to suggest to historians who he was.

While there is much about Sherman to admire, especially from the Union perspective, it must be admitted that there are troubling aspects of the man. While one must be careful not to evaluate a historical figure according to the culture and values of the twenty-first century, Sherman's attitudes on race are troubling in any era. He was not in tune with the liberals of his time. He avoided having African American troops in his armies, and disregarded voting rights for them at first. In many ways, his attitudes toward Native Americans were worse. African Americans at least had value as human beings, while he did not feel the same about Native Americans. His design to subjugate Native Americans through the destruction of the buffalo is thoroughly despicable.

On the professional side, Sherman has often been hailed or condemned as one of the inventors of total war. Historian Charles Edmund Vetter observed that "Successfully combining into his theory of war . . . three elements—the economic, the psychological, and the sociological—Sherman made the South and much of the Western world realize the effectiveness of "total war." Minimizing battle and jangling an opponent's nerves, sapping their willingness to fight, and demoralizing them became hallmarks of Sherman's war strategy. More psychological in nature, the "indirect approach" introduced a style of war with a "zero sum" character.

William T. Sherman after the war. Sherman was a very popular speaker at soldier reunions and relished the acclaim they brought him. (loc)

Sherman celebrated few militarily decisive battlefield victories. Yet, his innovations led to overall Union victory. He has been criticized down the years for avoiding battle and not destroying armies when it may have been in his power—Johnston's army at Bentonville, for example. His vision was larger. "Sherman calculated shrewdly that panic and exaggeration would do his job for him," historian Brian Holden Reid observed, "and he was proved right." Why waste lives when the object can be attained through maneuvering and breaking the Confederate will to fight, the general believed.

Sherman's place in history will always be a matter of argument. The complexities of his personality and military innovations will always give historians plenty to talk about. Clearly, though, Sherman was a passionate man, compelling and fascinating, loved and hated. In the end, it is hard to define Sherman. Then again, if he struggled to find his identity and place in the world for seventy years, it is no wonder that it should still be debated today.

The Missouri Civil War Museum at Jefferson Barracks in St. Louis tells the story of Sherman's time in the city. (kt)

Walking in Sherman's Footsteps: Prominent Sherman Historic Sites

APPENDIX A

By Derek D. Maxfield

William Tecumseh Sherman was a wanderer. He never stood still and was never satisfied in one place for long. The country is littered with Sherman way stations; sadly, many sites associated with the eccentric general have long since disappeared. The following sites are a mere sampling of places where the general left his mark.

The Sherman House

Dating to 1811, the Sherman House is the birthplace and early boyhood home of William Tecumseh Sherman. Judge Charles Sherman and his wife Mary (nee Hoyt) acquired and expanded the frame house before William's birth here in 1820. Operated now by the Fairfield Heritage Association, the site is available for tours.

The Sherman House Museum
137 East Main Street
Lancaster, Ohio 43130
Phone: 740-654-9923

Now the Sherman House Museum, this house is the birthplace of not only General William Tecumseh Sherman but also his brother Secretary John Sherman. (ddm)

The Ewing-Ryckman House

In 1824, Thomas Ewing purchased a lot just up the hill from his good friend Charles Sherman and proceeded to build a magnificent mansion. As the Ewing brood grew, so too did the house. New wings were added, and a high brick wall surrounded the property. William Tecumseh Sherman moved into the Ewing home at age nine, after the death of his father, Charles. The house and property are privately owned and are not open to the public.

The Ewing – Ryckman House
163 E. Main St.
Lancaster, Ohio 43130

The Old Ewing Homestead was built on land purchased by Secretary Thomas Ewing in Lancaster, Ohio, in 1824. (ddm)

General William Tecumseh Sherman Monument

This equestrian statue of General Sherman stands on the ground where once stood the reviewing stand for the famous Grand Review of Union armies in the closing days of the Civil War. Designed by Carl Rohl-Smith, but not completed until after his death, the monument was dedicated by President Theodore Roosevelt on October 15, 1903.

Dedicated in 1903, the Sherman equestrian monument sits near the White House in Sherman Plaza, Washington, D.C. (wc)

Sherman Plaza, President's Park
At the intersection of 15th Street NW,
Pennsylvania Avenue NW,
and Treasury Place NW
Washington, D.C.
GPS: 38°53′45.6″N 77°02′03.5″W

General Sherman's Grave

General Sherman died in Manhattan, New York City, on Valentine's Day—February 14, 1891, at 71. His wife Ellen (nee Ewing), a devout Catholic, was already interred in Calvary Cemetery, as were two of his sons. The ensuing funerary parade on February 21st from the railroad depot to the cemetery in St. Louis was a four-hour affair featuring over 12,000 troops, and "The greatest funeral pageant ever seen in the West." The general's son Rev. Thomas Sherman delivered brief remarks graveside and committed his father's remains. The epitaph on the stone was written by the eccentric redhead himself, "Faithful and Honorable."

After the Civil War, the Shermans were gifted a beautiful home in St. Louis, which was located at 912 N. Garrison Ave., but sadly the house was later destroyed.

Grave of William Tecumseh Sherman, Calvary Cemetery, St. Louis, MO. Founded just before the Civil War, this Roman Catholic bone yard now holds more than 300,000. (ddm)

Section 17 Lot 8
Calvary Cemetery
5239 West Florissant Avenue
Saint Louis, St. Louis City, Missouri, 63115-1460

General Sherman's Headquarters—Savannah

Located on Madison Square in beautiful Savannah, Georgia, the Green-Meldrim House is a magnificent Greek Revival-style home, built in 1853 for cotton merchant Charles Green. Shortly after the Union occupation of the city, Green offered his home to General Sherman for his headquarters. The general would make the house his home and headquarters for several weeks before the Carolinas campaign. A magnificent Christmas dinner was hosted by the general during his tenure with Green as a guest of honor.

The Green-Meldrim House is now owned by St. John's Episcopal Church, which offers occasional tours. Call (912) 232-1251 for more information.

Green–Meldrim House
14 W Macon St.
Savannah, GA 31401

General Sherman's headquarters in Savannah, Georgia, was established in the Green-Meldrim House on Madison Square. (ddm)

General Sherman's Headquarters—Milledgeville

This Greek Revival Mansion served as the home of Georgia's chief executives from 1838 until after the Civil War. But in November 1864, it was the temporary home of Union General William Tecumseh Sherman, who confiscated the property to use as his headquarters during his famous March

During Sherman's March to the Sea campaign, the general made his headquarters briefly at the Governor's Mansion in Milledgeville. Now a museum on the campus of Georgia College & State University, this Greek Revival-style building was opened in 1839. (loc)

to the Sea campaign. Today the mansion sits on the campus of Georgia College and State University and functions as a museum.

The Old Governor's Mansion is open for tours most days 10:00 am to 4:00 pm.

Old Governor's Mansion
120 S. Clark St.
Milledgeville, GA 31061

Louisiana State Seminary of Learning & Military Academy (Ruins)

The Louisiana State Seminary of Learning & Military Academy opened its doors in early January 1860 with five professors and just a handful of cadets. Happy to finally have found a job to his liking, Superintendent William Tecumseh Sherman was optimistic about his and the academy's prospects—though the clouds of war were gathering. The original academy building was destroyed by fire in 1869, and the school moved to Baton Rouge, where it was rechristened Louisiana State University.

The remains of the original building mark the location of the original Louisiana State Seminary of Learning & Military Academy. (wc)

801-999 Maryhill Rd.
Pineville, LA 71360
GPS: 31°21'31"N 92°26'14"W

William Tecumseh Sherman and Victory Monument

Dedicated in 1903 on the Southeast corner of Central Park in Manhattan, the gilded Sherman monument was designed and sculpted by Augustus Saint-Gaudens. According to the Central Park Conservancy, "The monument depicts Sherman on his horse, Ontario, led by the allegorical figure of Victory ... The figure of Victory is depicted crushing a palm frond, a symbol of the south, in her hand as she leads Sherman to Union victory."

East Side and 60th St.
at Grand Army Plaza
New York, New York 10022
GPS: 40.7645°N 73.9732°W

The William Tecumseh Sherman and Victory Monument in Manhattan is now a controversial landmark—with some calling to remove the monument due to Sherman's reputation for racism.
(wc)

Fort Moultrie

Named for General William Moultrie, a Revolutionary War veteran, Fort Moultrie is a set of fortifications on Sullivan's Island near Charleston, South Carolina. During the Civil War, Major Robert Anderson, in command of the 1st U.S. Artillery, moved his garrison from Moultrie to the more secure location at Fort Sumter in Charleston Harbor.

William Tecumseh Sherman, then a Lieutenant, was stationed at Fort Moultrie for four years beginning in 1842, where he became close friends with Anderson. Often away on special assignments during these years, Sherman enjoyed his time in South Carolina.

1214 Middle Street
Sullivan's Island, SC 29482

Fort Moultrie, Sullivan's Island, near Charleston, South Carolina, was originally named Fort Sullivan. (loc)

Bennett Place

Site of Confederate General Joseph E. Johnston's surrender to Union general William Tecumseh Sherman, the Bennett Farm in Durham is now a state historic site. Following word of Robert E. Lee's surrender to Ulysses S. Grant at Appomattox Court House, Virginia, Johnston was convinced that it was time for the Confederacy to fold. Confederate President Jefferson Davis disagreed. Johnston contacted Sherman anyway and opened negotiations to surrender his army. While Union authorities rejected the terms Sherman originally offered Johnston, the final surrender was based on the terms Grant offered Lee. The business was concluded April 26, 1865.

4409 Bennett Memorial Rd.
Durham, NC 27705
919-383-4345
Tuesday – Saturday 9 a.m. – 5 p.m.
Closed Sunday, Monday, and most major holidays
Admission is free

Home of James and Nancy Bennett, the farm in Durham, NC, became the site of the surrender of Confederate General Joe Johnston to William Tecumseh Sherman in 1865. (ddm)

Lucas, Turner & Co. (Sherman's Bank)

After many years of pestering, Ellen Ewing Sherman finally convinced her husband to leave the army. Sherman accepted the management of the San Francisco branch of Lucas, Turner & Co. bank. This building was opened to hold Sherman's bank in 1854 – just before a financial crisis tested the viability of the enterprise and the red-head's management abilities. Although the branch weathered the storm, the partners decided to close the branch in 1857.

494 Jackson St.
San Francisco, CA 94111

Site of Lucas, Turner, and Company's San Francisco bank, managed by William Tecumseh Sherman. (wc)

General Sherman's Quarters

In 1847, William Tecumseh Sherman made his quarters in this small adobe building, while supervising the construction of a fort at the Presidio. Now part of the Monterey State Historic Park, the building remained Sherman's home until 1849.

464 Calle Principal
Monterey, CA 93940
GPS: N 36° 35.844 W 121° 53.785

For about two years, Sherman made his quarters in this small house which now sits on the grounds of the Monterey State Historic Park. (wc)

Sherman's Shiloh Headquarters

Site of General Sherman's headquarters at the Shiloh National Military Park. Marker can be reached from the intersection of Corinth Road and Hamburg-Purdy Rd., on the left when traveling south—300 yards south of crossroads on a trail in the woods.

Shiloh National Military Park
Shiloh, TN 38376
GPS: 35° 8.098'N, 88° 21.154'W
For park hours and tour information call:
(731) 689-5696

This monument marks the location of Sherman's headquarters during the battle of Shiloh. (wc)

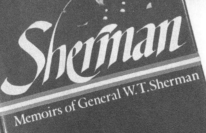

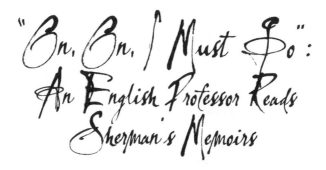

"On, On, I Must Go":
An English Professor Reads
Sherman's Memoirs

APPENDIX B

BY R. MICHAEL GOSSELIN

The only person known to have stopped William Tecumseh Sherman in his tracks was one Eliza Dean, a resident of St. Louis. Early in 1861, Sherman lived in that city close to Camp Jackson. The Camp, according to Sherman, was "nominally a state camp of instruction, but, beyond doubt . . . in the interest of the Southern cause." On May 9, the Camp came under attack by national authorities, and Miss Dean, Sherman's neighbor, expressed concern that one of her relatives serving in the camp would be killed. Sherman told her not to worry, that the force assaulting the camp would be sufficient to cause its quick surrender. "She would not be comforted," he writes, "saying that the camp was made up of the young men from the first and best families of St. Louis, and that they were proud, and would fight. I explained that young men of the best families did not like to be killed better than ordinary people." In the event, Sherman was right. But then he did the most Shermanesque thing imaginable: he crossed to Eliza Dean's house, knocked on her door, and delivered the news—in person. Not surprisingly, "[S]he angrily slammed the door in my face!"

That final exclamation point serves as a tantalizing window into Sherman's character. At first glance, it would seem to reveal a wounded vanity, not to mention a dash of sexism. The war, after all, had not even begun in earnest. However, by that date, Sherman had already served in Florida after graduating from West Point, traveled back and forth to California a few times (by ship!), ridden his horse all over the territory while there, and traveled to Baton Rouge to open the Louisiana Seminary of Learning and Military Academy. Who was he to be peremptorily shut down by a "Miss" anybody?

Sherman's memoirs have remained readable and accessible—and in print—since their original publication. (ck)(cm)

I believe, though, there is a different, more complex cause. In the essay "Living Like Weasels," American writer Annie Dillard tells of a man who once shot an eagle out of the sky. In the throat of the eagle was affixed the desiccated skull of a weasel. "The supposition," writes Dillard, "is that the eagle

Lt. Gen. John Bell Hood would go on to father eleven children after the war, including three sets of twins. (loc)

had pounced on the weasel and the weasel swiveled and bit as instinct taught him, tooth to neck. . . ." That was Sherman's instinct, too. Once drawn into a conflict, either of arms or words, he simply refused to let go. In a word, he was relentless. Eliza Dean had the good sense to slam the door on him, saving her neck.

General John Bell Hood was not so lucky. After Sherman ordered the evacuation of Atlanta in 1864, Hood sent him an overwrought letter chock full of grievances—not uncommon in Confederate rhetoric. Hood's letter claims that, among other things, the order was "unprecedented" and "transcends, in studied and ingenious cruelty, all acts ever before brought to my attention in the dark history of war," a statement that the citizens of the German city of Magdeburg, for instance, might have found ironic after the slaughter of 20,000 of its civilians during the Thirty Years War. Sherman, true to form, was furious and wrote to Henry Halleck in Washington that he "could not tamely submit to such impertinence."

Actually, being in complete control of the situation, he probably could. Sherman needn't have said anything. Alternately, he could have responded tersely, as Grant did to General Buckner at Fort Donelson, in the brief message that earned Grant the nickname "Unconditional Surrender." He also could have fallen back on the old Roman dictum, *Vae victis*—"Woe to the Conquered." But that would not be our Sherman. Instead, like Dillard's weasel, he "swiveled and bit." For me, the most remarkable section of the *Memoirs*, he engaged Hood in a war of letters, totaling, on Sherman's part, almost 2500 words. (One of these letters, amusingly enough, is signed, "Yours in haste . . . .") Even the famous Sherman dictum, "War is cruelty and you cannot refine it," is buried in an epistle of over 1000 words.

On the other hand, the final letter in the series contains what might be the shortest sentence in the entire *Memoirs* and perhaps in all of Sherman's oeuvre: "I was not bound by the laws of war to give notice of the shelling of Atlanta, a 'fortified town, with magazines, arsenals, foundries, and public stores;' you were bound to take notice. See the books." It meant, that he was done talking, and he closed out the entire exchange by writing, "This is the conclusion of our correspondence, which I did not begin, and terminate with satisfaction." Slam. Eliza Dean would have approved.

Sherman's relentless energy is manifest in more than these verbal artillery duels. As Michael Fellman, Professor of History at Simon Fraser University, writes in the Introduction to the Penguin Classics edition of the *Memoirs*, "[W]hen Grant came to write his elegantly crafted memoirs … he wrapped his cloak of reserve and taciturnity tightly around his innermost feelings, while Sherman, though he of course camouflaged many memories, could not help but burst out in self-display far more candid and grandiose than was the Victorian norm." Such bursting is evident immediately. Grant's *Memoirs* opens with the famously succinct line, "My family is American, and has been for generations, in all its branches, direct and collateral." Here's Sherman, right out of the gate:

> *According to Cothren, in his "History of Ancient Woodbury, Connecticut," the Sherman family came from Dedham, Essex County, England. The first recorded name is of Edmond Sherman, with his three sons, Edmond, Samuel, and John, who were at Boston before 1636; and farther it is distinctly recorded that Hon. Samuel Sherman, Rev. John, his brother, and Captain John, his first cousin, arrived from Dedham, Essex County, England, in 1634. Samuel afterward married Sarah Mitchell, who had come (in the same ship) from England, and finally settled at Stratford, Connecticut. The other two (Johns) located at Watertown, Massachusetts.*

That's nearly 100 words, with 21 commas, two sets of parentheses, and a semicolon.

Later, in Chapter XIII, another letter to Halleck tops out at over 3,400 words. One paragraph reveals Sherman's eagerness to prosecute the war to the bitter end and foreshadows the tactics—and the ideology—behind the March to The Sea:

> *I would banish all minor questions, assert the broad doctrine that as a nation the United States has the right, and also the physical power, to penetrate to every part of our national domain, and that we will do it— that we will do it in our own time and in our own way; that it makes no difference whether it be in one year, or two, or ten, or twenty; that we will remove and destroy every obstacle, if need be, take every life, every acre of land, every particle of property, everything that to us seems proper; that we will not cease till the end is*

attained; that all who do not aid us are enemies, and that we will not account to them for our acts.

If you're keeping score, that's one sentence, 129 words, 13 commas, four semicolons, and an em dash, not to mention seven "that's." The headlong charge is exhilarating.

A third example—perhaps the most poetic passage in the book—describes the scene when the Fourteenth Corps marched out of Atlanta on its long march through Georgia:

Behind us lay Atlanta, smouldering and in ruins, the black smoke rising high in air, and hanging like a pall over the ruined city. Away off in the distance . . . was the rear of Howard's column, the gun barrels glistening in the sun, the white-topped wagons stretching away to the south; and right before us the Fourteenth Corps, marching steadily and rapidly, with a cheery look and swinging pace, that made light of the thousand miles that lay between us and Richmond. Some band, by accident, struck up the anthem of "John Brown's soul goes marching on;" the men caught up the strain, and never before or since have I heard the chorus of "Glory, glory, hallelujah!" done with more spirit, or in better harmony of time and place. Then we turned our horses' heads to the east; Atlanta was soon lost behind the screen of trees, and became a thing of the past.

But enough. When it comes to inspirational rhetoric, the *Memoirs* is an embarrassment of riches.

It must be noted, however, that all does not appear to be well with Sherman. There is a certain dissociative quality to some of his language, a feeling that he considered himself merely a pawn in the hands of an external power, or the victim of other people's actions, and not at all responsible for the actions—occasionally savage by our standards—that marked his time in the army, both during and after the War. The objective pronouncement that "war is cruelty" is only the most salient example. Another is his note to Halleck claiming that he "could not" submit to Hood's "impertinence." It also contains his answer to complaints about the forced evacuation of Atlanta: "If the people raise a howl against my barbarity and cruelty, I will answer that war is war, and not popularity-seeking. If they want peace, they and their relatives must stop the war." Finally, he ends the *Memoirs* with a line from Shakespeare:

Sherman was in high spirits as he left Atlanta. In his memoirs he relished the singing of the troops as they marched along. (wc)

"[A]s 'all the world's a stage, And all the men and women merely players,' I claim the privilege to ring down the curtain." What is not so final, though, is the question of who was directing the play.

Derek Maxfield, in the conclusion to this book, writes that Sherman "was driven to prove himself—to Thomas Ewing, to Union authorities, to the public, but most of all to himself," and he calls Sherman "haunted." Likewise, the General himself, in a touching letter after the death of his young son, Willie, wrote, "For myself I ask no sympathy. On, on I must go, to meet a soldier's fate. . . . " *On, on I must go*, to find . . . what, exactly? In a way, Grant and Sherman embodied different aspects of the American story: on the one hand, the reserved and efficient "plain businessman of the Republic," and on the other, the restless spirit, at once vengeful and haunted, searching, in a never-ending quest, for an identity made manifest in motion. As Walt Whitman wrote in *Leaves of Grass*,

O to die advancing on!

Are there some of us to droop and die? has the hour come?

Then upon the march we fittest die, soon and sure the gap is fill'd,

Pioneers! O pioneers!

In the end, perhaps Eliza Dean did not stop Sherman, but merely channeled that energy away from her door, where it could, like the Mississippi outside Vicksburg, find a wider course.

R. Michael Gosselin is an associate professor of English at Genesee Community College.

Becoming Sherman

APPENDIX C

BY TRACY FORD

I was just shy of 50 years old when I smoked my first cigar. I was on a little saddle connecting Culp's Hill and Cemetery Hill on the Gettysburg battlefield. I was puffing away awkwardly, and staring at the horizon in the dusk of day 1 of my first-ever visit to this humbling memorial to what is arguably our nation's gravest wound. However, I must admit that while I was appropriately contemplative and somber as I smoked, my mind was not entirely on the events that had taken place on the field over a century and a half earlier. I was indeed seeking a period rush, but I was focused on the mind of a man not present in Gettysburg in early July of 1863.

The author of this biography you now hold had asked me to portray William Tecumseh Sherman in a two-man show. Professor Maxfield would be Grant. We would stage a conversation between these two great generals, between these two friends. The location and date of their meeting were well known and well documented: City Point, Virginia—in late March of 1865. We would present a talk around the campfire the night before the famous meeting with President Lincoln aboard the *River Queen*. This campfire-Sherman would need to be a Sherman at his ease (as much as one can imagine that of WTS). A Sherman who had already come through (and certainly lit) most of the fire that would mark his Civil War career. He would be full of ideas about closing out the war, and full of stories about his marching and maneuvering and martial machinations, his correspondence with Hood over the disposition of Atlanta, and his bummers. This would need to be a confident Sherman and a congenial Sherman. This would need to be a three-dimensional Sherman.

Derek Maxfield (left) as Gen. Ulysses S. Grant and Tracy Ford (right) as Gen. William Tecumseh Sherman. The pair toured the country with a play titled *Now We Stand by Each Other Always.* (gcc)

In preparation for this part, I had begun amassing a Sherman library. I had purchased and burrowed into over 20 volumes—including his memoir and correspondence, famous and seminal biographies, and new and contrarian biographies—before I realized I was in over my head. As I'm sure all are aware, 20 books on Sherman represents a fraction of what has been written about the man. Lost in details and competing portraits, I needed a foothold. I needed a small truth or observation about the man, a hook, an anchor.

In bewilderment, I turned to the helpful guidance of a former professor of evolutionary biology turned communication specialist, Dr. Randy Olson. Olson offers a famous quote from 20th-century evolutionary biologist Theodosius Dobzhansky: "Nothing in biology makes sense except in the light of evolution." Modifying this statement as a tool to bring singular focus to an investigation, Olson suggests filling in blanks: "Nothing in _____ makes sense except in the light of _____." So I set to work trying to fill in the blanks.

Nothing in Sherman makes sense except in the light of _____? Obviously, the first blank was easy, but in searching for a fitting fill-in for the second, I had to turn back to fish in the sea of notions I had been confronted with after all my reading. I started a sort of process of elimination, and I started small. Cigars. Nothing in Sherman makes sense except in the light of cigars (because Sherman smoked his fair share, and the additional fair shares of two men and a small boy). Yes, I knew that was not the key, but I also knew that as an asthmatic who had avoided tobacco products my entire life, I at least needed to understand what it was to hold a cigar. I needed to look natural with one. I began carrying one everywhere. I taught with one in my hand—unlit, of course—gesticulating vigorously as I imagined an agitated Sherman might. I discovered that very cheap cigars fall apart rapidly— and knowing Sherman would not have tolerated cheap cigars—I moved to something sturdier: I wrapped brown paper around a permanent marker. The experiment continued, and I added to my already healthy reputation as an eccentric, a fitting detail for Sherman as well, if you come to that. After becoming proficient in handling the cigar, it was time to take my skills on the road. This is how it was that I found myself, under Professor Maxfield's careful guidance, smoking my first cigar at Gettysburg.

However, a cigar does not make a man. It is a prop. Granted, it is an important prop, but I could not very well rest with "Nothing in Sherman makes sense except in the light of cigars." Reminding myself that I needed to become a three-dimensional Sherman, I

Tracy Ford often practiced holding a cigar with a magic marker. (ddm)

began to react against the things that kept Sherman two-dimensional in the minds of so many casual students of history. Peering at all those typical 19th-century portraits of the man, I could only see him as pinched and colorless. It was too easy to read into those pictures the myth of the pillaging pyromaniacal villain promulgated by the Lost Causers. There was nothing to indicate his well-documented nervous energy nor his oft-noted red hair. There was no window into his sometimes puckish nature, nothing to expose the slightly unruly West Point cadet who would flout regulations to cook in his room and sneak off to a local bar at night. There was no trace, in those constipated black and white pictures of the man recent biographer Robert O'Connell likened to Daffy Duck with a machine-gun mouth (*Fierce Patriot*), a man who loved the theater and who quoted Shakespeare and Dickens in his memoir.

These bits of three-dimensionality point to Sherman's complexity, to his humanity. And that's where I began to fill in the blank in a useful way: "Nothing in Sherman makes sense except in the light of his humanity." Though this seems a painfully obvious and not overly insightful distillation, it put me in just the right frame of mind. This was not a character in a book; this was a quirky human, as we are all quirky humans. I determined I would walk on stage and make him a real person.

By the time of our first performance, I had only the basics locked in. I could handle a cigar, I had dyed my hair and beard red, I could move in the quick and animated manner Sherman was known for, I could gesticulate nervously and broadly, and I could fill a stage space with energy and noise. However, I was not Sherman yet. I would learn to grow into and with the part. During the Q&A after that first performance, Professor Maxfield told the audience that he had not had to look far for his Sherman. I was tall enough, loud enough, and jumpy enough to be just right for the part. We began to joke about typecasting, and in subsequent Q&A sessions after other performances, I began to roll with it, often telling folks that they weren't seeing Sherman up there on the stage; they were seeing me as a ginger in a Civil War major general's uniform.

Helpfully, and I suppose unsurprisingly, it was the questions from our audience which allowed me to hone in on his humanity. I had originally imagined that Professor Maxfield, the qualified historian, would field the bulk of the questions. The folks in the crowd were almost always Civil War enthusiasts. They had detailed and technical questions. Troop movements, strategies, War Department infighting—these were things I left to the history prof. Frequently, Lost Cause misconceptions of Sherman would pop up, and he would put them to rest in a scholarly way. However, sometimes he would hand them off to me. In those moments of rabbit-in-the-headlights panic, I would swallow hard and scramble for the few facts that stuck in my head from all that reading, but because at the end of the day, I, too, am a teacher, who just loves to hear himself talk, I would launch into what had become my thesis about the man. It was my goal to emphasize his humanity, to make him more than a prominent piece in an elaborate tabletop game for which almost everyone in the audience had a predetermined and largely immutable sense of the rules and of who exactly the players were. I would openly explain that I was still trying to understand the man, relate to him, and relate him to each audience.

Simple issues—simple questions—were instructive, and obviously not simple: Was Sherman racist? Yup. Such a question was not something that we just brushed past with, "Well, he was a man of his times." This offered a chance to tell stories, stories about Sherman's cranky dismissal of the value of African American troops, but also stories about the undeniable respect he showed to African American people in numerous anecdotes to be plucked from his biographies. And these moments of human complexity, three-dimensionality, had me reflecting on my own life, my own inconsistencies and contradictions, and on those same habits and tendencies among my closest friends and family. Don't you have a great uncle who is kind to all who meet him, regardless of their race or walk of life, yet after a glass of wine and a turkey leg at Thanksgiving, his frighteningly unenlightened views on race relations make you turtle into the neck of your sweater?

Such personal reflection meant personal connection, and not just in terms of understanding the big issues like Sherman's ideas on race. Little things fell into place. Sherman was an asthmatic too. Sherman lived in California during the gold rush, only an hour from where I grew up. I breathed the climate he breathed; I saw the land he saw. In stories of his late-night asthma attacks brought on by stress and anxiety, I felt the tightness in my chest. In his worry over making his way in the world, in providing for a growing family, I felt his fear. In his early Civil War career, his direct request to Lincoln that he not be put in command of an entire army made me aware of how I was always eager to be second banana, worried that I might precipitate disaster were I to be leading upfront. These links to Sherman made me aware of how intimately familiar I was with him. And ironically, just as the Grant and Sherman friendship and conduct of the war gave a growing confidence to Sherman, our Grant and Sherman production gave me a growing confidence. I found myself in Sherman, and Sherman in me. I became Cump, but not in the sense of inhabiting a role. I centered on his complexity and his relatable contradictions, on his humor and his passion and his fiery gusto, on his humanity. I discovered that nothing makes sense in William Tecumseh Sherman except in the light of me, of us, as quirky and complicated and impossible to sum up in a black and white picture or even a 300-page biography.

TRACY FORD **is an associate professor of English at Genesee Community College.**

Reckoning with the General:
Sherman in American Memory

APPENDIX D

BY JESSICA A. MAXFIELD

If you want a quick litmus test to determine someone's relationship to the Civil War, try throwing out the name "William Tecumseh Sherman." Depending on where you are in the United States, the mere mention of Sherman's name is enough to engender a glowering scowl, or a lip curled into a grimace from those who still hold Sherman responsible for the fiery destruction wrought across Georgia and the Carolinas. There is perhaps no other figure in the war which, to this day, elicits the same visceral emotional response.

The vilification of General Sherman is one of the defining features of his legacy. In his 1866 survey of the Southern landscape after the war, journalist Sidney Andrews wrote, "Whatever else the South Carolina mothers forget, they do not seem likely in this generation to forget to teach their children to hate Sherman." Later generations seem to have followed suit. To this day, Sherman-bashing is a longstanding tradition, that has deep roots in Southern lore and identity.

But this hatred is not universal. There is another Sherman in American memory. Sherman, the Union war hero. Sherman, the tactician. Sherman, the architect of modern warfare. This is the infinitely quotable "Uncle Billy" who waged total war against the Confederacy. Evidenced in the numerous monuments and historical sites across the country dedicated to his memory, this Sherman continues to be one of the most recognizable and popular figures of the Civil War.

Both of these Shermans, of course, are heavily influenced by myth. And both contribute to the legacy of destruction tied to his name. Cyclically eclipsing each other as the years pass, these competing versions of Sherman make up the bulk of how he is remembered. In recent years, however, a third view has emerged as we attempt to demystify Sherman's legacy and reckon with his role in American history. Sherman's memory is as complex as the man himself, and it is inseparable from the emotional investment people have made in efforts to celebrate him, demonize him, critique him, and, ultimately, identify with him.

One word says it all: "Sherman!" Historian Dan Davis talks about Sherman in memory as influenced by *Gone with the Wind* at an Emerging Civil War Symposium. (cm)

Sherman and his March are bound together in historical memory. One is rarely mentioned without the other. Sentimental stories of the March circulated during and long after the war, both from Union veterans, who prided themselves on subjugating the South and "making Georgia howl," and former Confederates who claimed to have resisted them. The March to the Sea became a tale of Union excess. Dramatized in typical nineteenth century fashion, the army feasted on the rich bounty of the South, destroying railroads and burning cities along the way. Sherman was the ringleader of this circus. While he detested the spin put on him by journalists, Sherman played into these myths by embellishing upon his deeds during his postwar tours of the U.S. and Europe.

While "Uncle Billy" was wildly popular among West Point cadets and future army recruits who lauded him as a hero and retold his tales of retribution, Sherman downplayed the significance of the March in his memoirs. This added to the criticism wielded against him by Northern journalists, who accused him of not being harsh enough on the South and even questioned his loyalty to the Union. Many who knew Sherman, Grant included, came to his defense. The popularity of Grant's memoirs cemented Sherman's March to the Sea as a key component of Union victory, and while its significance may be debated by scholars, it would remain to this day a fixture in American memory of the Civil War.

If Sherman burned his way into American memory during the March to the Sea, it was the hatred of Southern white women toward him in the years following the war that immortalized him. In their letters and diaries, Confederate women made Sherman out to be a murderer and a harbinger of death and destruction, placing the blame solely on him for the extent to which his army, his so-called "bummers," ravaged the landscape. Calling him "Prince of Bummers" and worse, for these women, Sherman embodied the victimization of the Southern people at the hands of the Union Army. It was beside the point that other venues of the war were just as destructive, or that excessive violence was perpetrated by both sides. The destruction of Sherman's March was felt by Southerners in a way that fundamentally changed their identity relative to the war.

Wherever Sherman's army went, droves of African American slaves swarmed to his force looking to effect their own freedom. (loc)

So it happened that hatred of Sherman became one of the pillars of the Lost Cause. While emotional investment in the Lost Cause would wane as time went on, many attribute its revival and staying power in the twentieth century to the influence of *Gone with the Wind*. Margaret Mitchell's book and the 1939 film of the same name portray an idealized antebellum culture torn asunder by the "screaming tornado" of Sherman and his men—quite literally gone with the wind.

The power of film to teach Americans their own history has long been lamented by historians. Film is a visually visceral medium. It immerses the viewer in an alternate reality, one in which images, sounds, music, even the narrative structure are all purposefully designed to evoke an emotional response. As Anne Sarah Rubin aptly points out in her book *Through the Heart of Dixie: Sherman's March and American Memory*, Sherman is not featured as a character in *Gone with the Wind*. He appears neither on page nor on screen. Instead, his is a presence that is felt and feared, more form than reality. The myth of the terrible Sherman supersedes the reality of the man.

A new refrain revived among Southern Civil War historians during this period was that Sherman's March accomplished little more than wanton violence against an already demoralized and humiliated Southern people. These interpretations were poorly veiled attempts to downplay the significance of the March in securing Union victory, while holding Sherman singularly responsible.

In the second half of the twentieth century, a different Sherman would emerge to contradict these claims. This Sherman stemmed from the work of British military historians, especially B. H. Liddell Hart, who revisited Sherman's contributions to the war and placed his significance in the context of global war studies. Liddell Hart famously argued that Sherman waged total war against the South, a strategy he and Grant learned in the Western Theatre. This left an indelible stamp on historiography. For the next thirty to forty years, Sherman was lauded by historians for his military prowess. Words like "genius" and "prophet" colored these interpretations.

But while Sherman's March blurred the line between home front and battlefront, and between combatants and noncombatants, later scholars, like Mark Grimsley and Mark E. Neely, Jr., argued that

B. H. Liddell Hart, more properly known as Sir Basil Henry Liddell Hart, was a Captain of light artillery in World War I and became a noted military historian. (loc)

this was no different than in other venues of the war, that it did not constitute "total war" in the modern sense of the phrase. Neely went as far as to argue that the Union Army practiced a level of restraint against the Confederate Army, one which, he emphasized, was not extended to the Plains Indians. Following Grimsley's lead, total war became hard war, and Sherman's reputation was once again up for debate.

Historian Arthur Schlesinger, Jr. once said, "When new urgencies arise in our own times and lives, the historian's spotlight shifts, probing now into the darkness, throwing into sharp relief things that were always there but that earlier historians had carelessly excised from the collective memory. New voices ring out of the historical darkness and demand attention."

If Sherman's military record left him open to critique in the 20th century, the spotlight of history would shift once again going into the 21st. This time criticism would not be wielded by those immersed in Lost Cause mythology, but by modern historians seeking to illuminate the narratives of the average person during the war rather than rehash the focus on the war's key figures. Revisiting the fragmented records of formerly enslaved refugees, Southern women, and the indigenous peoples of the Great Plains and Southwestern United States, many Civil War scholars have continued the debate over the extent of the war's destruction and Sherman's role in it—from the lens of the people it affected rather than the perpetrators.

It has long been known that Sherman was both a racist and a colonizer. These are not new criticisms. His treatment of Black refugees and his role in the wars against the Plains Indians famously attest to this. However, coming to terms with the reality of his racism reveals to us the stories hidden underneath—those of the people who reacted to him, who felt things about him, and who were impacted by him. Illuminating this darker side of Sherman's legacy gives us new stories of Southern women, who wrote extensively of their plight and who actively protested their conditions, of the tens of thousands of enslaved people who risked everything to follow Sherman's army to freedom, and of the indigenous people who negotiated and fought for their sovereignty in the face of colonization.

Political cartoon which appeared in *Leslie's Illustrated* highlights Sherman's role in Indian policy. (loc)

Sherman's name carries with it the weight of suffering and destruction in a way that other figures of the war do not. It colors every word written about him, every iteration of his character. Knowing this,

Sherman is noticeably absent in much of the new scholarship on the Civil War, featured instead as a figure looming in the background. Unlike in *Gone with the Wind*, where this served to amplify the terror surrounding him, here it serves to diffuse it. Rather than simply condemning Sherman, other figures and institutions emerge in need of analysis. The age of Sherman the scapegoat begins to give way to accountability for all.

History's band-aid is being removed from Sherman's legacy. What this approach means for Sherman in popular memory remains to be seen, but one thing is certain, he will not be forgotten. Sherman's reputation has a phoenix-like quality, and this perhaps stems from his complexity. He is, in many ways, all things to all people. Fans and critics alike find themselves in the stories surrounding him. Sherman's humanity acts as a mirror—whether this reflects a sense of pride, a sense of shame, or a sense of identity is up to interpretation.

As historian Drew Gilpin Faust has suggested, we who read about and study the Civil War do not do so necessarily because of the war's significance, we do so because the stories and people of that time resonate with us. For better or worse, we see ourselves reflected in them. Through these stories, we learn a little bit about who we are, and who we could be.

Perhaps this is why so many find themselves drawn to Sherman, even if they hate him. It is a myth in itself that Sherman is universally hated in the South. In *Through the Heart of Dixie*, Anne Sarah Rubin wrote about the many travelers who have trekked Sherman's March long after the war. Today, following the path of Sherman and his men is a means of self-discovery and connectedness with history. Even removed by over one hundred years, Sherman's influence is threaded not just through American memory, but through our experience of the past in the present.

Sherman's story is of a complex man whose outspoken conviction, ingenuity, humor, and passion stay with us, even as we periodically reconsider his reputation and role in history. Regardless of how we feel about Sherman, and whether his memory is cast in a positive or negative light, we can say assuredly that the spotlight of history will, from time to time, fall on Sherman. His memory is ineradicably stamped into American history. How we reckon with that history is up to us.

JESSICA A. MAXFIELD **is a reference librarian at Genesee Community College.**

Sherman: A Soldier's Passion for Order
John F. Marszalek
Free Press, 1993
ISBN: 978-0-02920-135-0

Once considered the definitive biography of Sherman, this book nonetheless is where everyone interested in Sherman should start. Well-written and researched, Marszalek's book puts Sherman's need for order front and center as the central theme of the book.

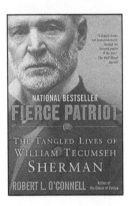

Fierce Patriot: The Tangled Lives of William Tecumseh Sherman
Robert O'Connell
Random House, 2014
ISBN: 978-1-40006-972-9

This highly entertaining biography is a great book with a lot of character. O'Connell's colorful prose makes this biography a joy to read. Organized into three sections, O'Connell looks at different aspects of the general's life—instead of writing a standard chronological biography.

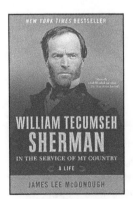

William Tecumseh Sherman: In the Service of My Country
James Lee McDonough
W. W. Norton & Company, 2016
ISBN: 978-0-39324-157-0

Some would say that McDonough's book is now the definitive biography of the redheaded general. This massive work is very detailed and exhaustively researched, though a bit of a slough to read. It ably shows an evolving, complex man who was eminently a social animal.

The Scourge of War: The Life of
William Tecumseh Sherman
Brian Holden Reid
Oxford University Press, 2020
ISBN: 978-0-19539-273-9

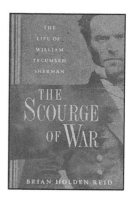

The newest full-length biography of Sherman,
Reid's book is highly recommended. A military
historian, Reid provides fresh insight into the lanky
general's battlefield tactics and military strategy
and tackles head-on the notion that Sherman was
the father of total war.

Sherman: Fighting Prophet
Lloyd Lewis
University of Nebraska Press, 1993
ISBN: 978-0-80327-945-2

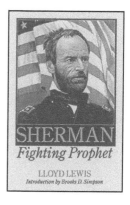

An older work, Lewis's biography has become a
classic. *Fighting Prophet* is a great narrative and a fun
read. Pulling together the contradictory elements
in Sherman's character, Lewis perceptively
demonstrates that this complex individual is a
deep, highly intellectual man who demonstrates a
good understanding of human nature.

Sherman: Merchant of Terror, Advocate of Peace
Charles Edmund Vetter
Pelican Publishing, 1992
ISBN: 978-0-88289-860-5

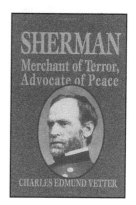

Not so much a biography of Sherman, Vetter's
Sherman: Merchant of Terror, Advocate of Peace seeks
to define the erratic general's philosophy of war
and place his reputation in a historical context.
A professor of sociology and military history in
Louisiana, Vetter has an interest in demonstrating
Sherman's love of the South, which did not change
with the war. The portrait painted by Vetter
shows a complex man who evolved with the war,
developing new strategy and tactics foreshadowing
modern warfare.

About the Author

Derek Maxfield is an associate professor of history at Genesee Community College in Batavia, New York. Author of *Hellmira: The Union's Most Infamous Civil War Prison Camp—Elmira, NY,* Maxfield has written for Emerging Civil War since 2015. In 2019, he was honored with the SUNY Chancellor's Award for Excellence in Teaching, and in 2013, he was awarded the SUNY Chancellor's Award for Excellence in Scholarship and Creative Activities.